CROSSCURRENTS
PURSUING SOCIAL JUSTICE AND INTERRELIGIOUS WORK
SINCE 1950

CrossCurrents (ISSN 0011-1953; online ISSN 1939-3881) connects the wisdom of the heart with the life of the mind and the experiences of the body. The journal is operated through its parent organization, the Association for Public Religion and Intellectual Life (APRIL), an interreligious network of academics, activists, artists, and community leaders seeking to engage the many ways religion meets the public. Contributions to the journal exist at the nexus of religion, education, the arts, and social justice. The journal is published quarterly on behalf of the Association for Public Religion and Intellectual Life by the University of North Carolina Press.

The Association for Public Religion and Intellectual Life (formerly ARIL) is a global network of leaders, scholars, and social change agents who explore religious life, engage in intellectual inquiry, and lead ethical action in the world today. Their primary objective, especially through annual summer colloquia and *CrossCurrents*, is to bring together leading voices of our time to advocate for justice and to examine global spiritual and interreligious currents in both historical and contemporary perspectives.

A membership to APRIL includes access to *CrossCurrents* starting with Volume 58, 2008, though our partners at Project MUSE, monthly newsletters, early access to summer colloquium themes, a 40% on UNC Press books, and more. For more information, including membership and subscription rates, visit www.aprilonline.org.

This reissue of *CrossCurrents* was one of four issues published in 2012 as part of Volume 62. For a current masthead visit www.aprilonline.org.

© 2012 Association for Public Religion and Intellectual Life. All rights reserved.

ISBN 978-1-4696-6673-0 (Print)

CROSSCURRENTS

VOLUME 62, NO 3 ISSN 0011-1953

DIFFICULT DIALOGUES

298
Editorial
Katharina von Kellenbach

301
The Art of Dialogue:
Jewish–Christian Relations in a Post-Shoah World
(The Jerome Cardin Memorial Lecture)
Björn Krondorfer

318
A different kind of dialogue?:
Messianic Judaism and Jewish-Christian Relations
Yaakov Ariel

328
Encountering Habits of Mind at Table: Kashrut, Jews, and Christians
Lisa M. Hess

337
Who Speaks for Europe's Muslims?: The Radical Right Obstacle to Dialogue
Todd H. Green

350
I the Jew, I the Buddhist: Multi-Religious Belonging As Inner Dialogue
Mira Niculescu

360
Complex religious identity in the context of interfaith dialogue
Karla Suomala

371
Embodying Tradition
Liturgical Performance as a Site for Interreligious Learning
Emma O'Donnell

381
The nonduality of diversity: Dialogue Among Religious Traditions
Grace Song

389
Notes on Contributors

EDITORIAL

Katharina von Kellenbach

In July 2011, a group of scholars attended the ARIL Coolidge Research Colloquium in New York City to explore the *Intersection of Religious Pluralism and Jewish–Christian Dialogue*. The conveners, Karla Suomala, Bjorn Krondorfer, and myself are members of the Christian Scholars Group (CSG) on Jewish–Christian Relations, an academic think tank that has been meeting since the late 1960s to conduct and promote research in the spirit of Jewish–Christian dialogue (http://www.ccjr.us/members/christian-scholars-group). The Christian Scholars Group wanted to engage with newer scholarly projects in religious pluralism, comparative theology, and interfaith initiatives that have developed and grown in the last decades. We wondered whether Jewish–Christian dialogue had run its course and whether the intellectual passion and scholarly curiosity had shifted toward, say Jewish–Muslim dialogue and other forms of interreligious engagement. We had noticed a growing disconnect between the discourses on religious pluralism and comparative theology, which theorize and reflect on the changing landscape of religious belongings in a globalized world, on the one hand, and Jewish–Christian dialogue, which evolved in the aftermath of the devastation of the Holocaust and founding of the state of Israel, on the other. We had invited participants based on their scholarly project proposals and looked forward to the conversation.

This issue of *Crosscurrents* on *Difficult Dialogue* was solicited from colloquium participants (except for Todd Green) and reflects the diversity of the projects. In addition to sharing our scholarship, the colloquium participants engaged in a series of facilitated discussions that set out to define the basic terms that form the discursive field: comparative religions, comparative theology, theology of religions, interreligious dialogue, interfaith dialogue, religious pluralism, dual and multiple religious belonging, hybrid and hyphenated identities. It became evident quickly that this field has expanded rapidly and that new terms and categories were created faster than one could keep up and define. Even after spending a month trying to gain clarity, we could not trust that we were using a particular term correctly, or that there even was a correct way to use a certain concept. Our meta-discussions on interreligious dialogue, comparative theology and religious pluralism were confusing and sometimes tedious because we rarely went beyond initial rounds of clarification of terms and definitions of concepts. These more abstract sessions were interesting and informative but not truly engaging.

It was only when we turned to particular dialogues, say Christian–Buddhist dialogue, Christian–Muslim relations, or the internalized Jewish–Buddhist dialogue that the discussion would take off. In these particular dialogues, we were on firmer ground and could rely on concise terminology, concrete histories, and political settings. Still, Jewish–Christian dialogue remained *sui generis*. It was not at all a worn-out conversation between an old married couple but a passionate affair. These conversations were haunted by two thousand years of polemics, conversions, apologetics, disputations, appropriations, border enforcements, and border crossings. The theological differences and disparate perspectives still provoked debates, because the two traditions share basic theological concepts but use them differently, read the same sacred texts but interpret them disparately. When Jews and Christians meet, their religious identities are on the line. Jewish–Christian dialogue is threatening, not primarily because of what we learn about the other, but because of what we discover about ourselves.

The borderline between Judaism and Christianity is contested territory. When Protestant theologian Lisa Hess experimented with kashrut-observance in dialogue with Orthodox Jews, her Christian interpretation of Paul's letter to the Galatians had to change. When Messianic Jews blend Torah-observance and Jewish identity with evangelical Christian faith in Christ, the borderline is crossed. Although Jewish–Buddhists perform similar acts of blending, such hybridity appears less subversive and elicits less outrage and consternation. Buddhism is perceived as less of a menace, because it has been culturally removed and politically non-threatening. Its philosophies and practices are clearly distinct and can be integrated or rejected without endangering Jewish practice or Christian doctrine. Buddhism and Judaism have coexisted peaceably on parallel tracks, where Judaism and Christianity have intersected, challenged, questioned, answered, and engaged each other for centuries. Scholars engaged in Jewish–Christian dialogue have only recently revised this history of mutual contempt and begun to map the borderland of cross-fertilization.

If our experience during those four weeks is any indication, then it is the difficult dialogues that electrify the room. As long as interreligious dialogue and religious pluralism remain abstract, a disembodied practice and globalized vision, everybody nodded along. But the conversations came alive where the topic was loaded with meaning, complicated by misunderstandings, and fraught with politics and history. Clearly, only those dialogues are worth having that are difficult.

THE ART OF DIALOGUE
Jewish–Christian Relations in a Post-Shoah World
(The Jerome Cardin Memorial Lecture)[1]

Björn Krondorfer

We wish, perhaps, that some events of the past would quietly fall into oblivion, be erased from collective memory for a fresh start. Surely, the Holocaust, or Shoah, would be such an event: The systematic attempt of Nazi Germany and its European collaborators to annihilate all European Jews and Jewish culture revealed modernity's darkest side, and it sobered the Enlightenment's belief in the steady progress of humanity toward moral improvement. The unleashing of unprecedented genocidal violence was made possible by putting modern technology and a bureaucratic apparatus into the service of a nation state ruled by a racial ideology. What started in the early years of Hitler's dictatorship as domestic terror evolved into a systematic genocidal campaign after the beginning of World War II in 1939. In hundreds of camps dotting the European map, the so-called inferior and undesirable people labored, starved, suffered, and died. The abyss of this system of terror was reached when the six extermination camps started their operations in December of 1941. The name Auschwitz is seared into our collective conscience and consciousness.

When we think about Auschwitz, the term dialogue does not readily come to mind. Auschwitz, it seems, is the antithesis to dialogue, to understanding, to reconciliation, and to life. Philosopher Theodor Adorno once wondered whether poetry can be written again after Auschwitz, and we may similarly ask whether dialogue can happen again in the face of such calamity. Auschwitz, one might say, is a negative space, a cemetery without graves, a house of death without traces—and this negative vortex cannot be mended or undone by dialogue. But Auschwitz today is no longer a death camp: It has become a memorial site, a tourist site, and a site of modern pilgrimage of millions of visitors each year. And if Auschwitz the death camp dampens any optimism about the prospect of dialogue, Auschwitz the contemporary memorial site demands us to engage a dialogical ethics.

The importance of dialogue is the topic I want to address at this occasion. I want to show that there is an *art* to dialoguing, and this art calls us into an ethical commitment of relationality. I also want to show that the art to dialoguing involves, literally, the *arts*. In my life, I have experienced and practiced dialogue through the performance arts as well as the visual arts. The body of work that my artist friend Karen Baldner and I created over the years is one example of how the visual arts can facilitate dialogue and serve as a catalyst for restoration and transformation. Our collaborative effort (previously covered in *CrossCurrents*[2]) has resulted in multiple objects of installations, prints, and book art that serve as witnesses to our ongoing dialogue between a Jewish German woman and a non-Jewish German man, both of whom were raised in Germany but are now residing in the United States.

The Cardin Memorial Lecture has, over many years now, offered ample occasions to publicly reflect on aspects of Jewish–Christian relations, and so I start there as well. As much as I have emphasized in my opening words that the annihilation of European Jews must be understood as a genocidal effort of a *modern secular* dictatorship, it is also true that the silence and complicity of the Christian churches contributed to the utter abandonment of the Jewish communities during the Holocaust. Soon after 1945, however, this fatal neglect triggered a process of soul-searching among Christian communities and led to a thorough overhaul of Christian thinking about Judaism. Christians began to repudiate their anti-Judaic, anti-Jewish, and antisemitic traditions that have blinded and distorted their century-old views of Jews and the Jewish religion (Fig. 1).

In his 2011 volume on church documents of post-1945 Christian-Jewish dialogue, Lutheran theologian Franklin Sherman summarizes those changes succinctly. He writes: "A transformation has taken place in recent times in the relation between Christianity and Judaism."[3] Sherman dates the beginning of this transformation to February 1946, when the nascent World Council of Churches expressed a "deep sense of horror at

Figure 1. Detail. *pushmepullyou* (2007). Baldner and Krondorfer. Unique book (7" × 11" × ¼"). The page reads: "My Cultural Portfolio" and shows a sacrificial lamb (*Opferlamm*) on one side and, on the other, an antisemitic woodcut of the *Judensau*.

the unprecedented tragedy which has befallen the Jewish people" and acknowledged "the failure of the churches."[4] Christianity shed its supersessionist ideology that portrayed Judaism as inferior, as the old Israel, as God-killers, and so forth, and, instead, began to speak of Judaism and Christianity as sibling faith traditions. In 1948, the World Council of Churches followed up with the declaration that "antisemitism is a sin against God"[5]; and in 1965, the Catholic Church issued the authoritative *Nostra Aetate* (In Our Time), in which it repudiated the Christian teachings of contempt, affirmed God's covenant with the Jewish people, and declared the church's opposition to any "hatred" and "persecutions" directed against Jews.[6] For the past seven decades, efforts at improving Jewish–Christian relations through dialogue have been, to say the least, impressive. Despite occasional attempts to the contrary, there is little chance of turning back to pre-Holocaust theological attitudes that had declared Jews and Judaism the antithesis of Christianity.

That is not to say that all problems are resolved, which is far from it. Misinformation and misunderstanding continue to exist among Jews and Christians, and more work needs to be done on individual and parochial levels and concerning liturgical and lectionary reform. Much of this task, however, falls into educational efforts of effectively teaching the theological insights gained over the last decades to the parishioners in local churches and synagogues. The theological shift itself, however—this new paradigm of thinking about and going about Christian–Jewish relations—has irrevocably taken place, and ample evidence of this transformation is available in print, in the form of local committees and regional institutes, or in national and international organizations, such as the International Council of Christians and Jews or the Christian Scholars Group on Christian–Jewish Relations in Boston, of which I am a member.[7]

There is something comfortably undiluted and unambiguous in the particularity of a covenantal relationship affirmed in the post-1945 Jewish-Christian dialogue. The sculpture "Relatum-Silence" (1997–2007) by artist Lee Ufan evokes, for me at least, the clarity of such dialogue, even though Ufan, a Korean-born artist, steeped in Asian religious sentiments, intended something quite different with his art.[8] In "Relatum-Silence," a massive steel plate and heavy boulder are placed opposite each other, the plate towering over the rock in front of it, with some space between them. These two objects are in a narrative relationship, facing each other across an indeterminate space. They seem to tell a story of a face-to-face encounter of two identifiable entities, a rock and a steel plate, like Moses standing at the stony top of Mount Sinai in the face of God. They stand in a covenantal relation. Perhaps it is the moment of God's revelation to Moses, leaving as tangible evidence the stone tablet with the commandments. We could even imagine the rock and the plate to represent Christians and Jews in dialogue, intimately connected, yet separated by a space between them, one hard as a rock, the other firm as steel. There is both a tense as well as a contemplative aura to this relationship, a history of violence as well as a mystagogic intimacy.

If we imagine Jewish–Christian relations as represented in Lee Ufan's art, we must realize that the calm lucidity of his sculpture would be more broken and fragmented today because of the growing cacophony of diverse voices from around the globe. The image by artist Siona Benjamin (see front cover of this issue) captures for me, like no other painting, the contemporary challenge that religious indeterminacy poses to the covenantal particularity of Jewish-Christian dialogue. Siona Benjamin, a Sephardic Jew from India, combines in reverent and irreverent ways Christian, Jewish, and Muslim iconography, displaying also recognizable Holocaust signs and a heightened gender sensibility. Imitating Jewish and

Christian illuminated manuscripts and Indian miniature paintings from the Mughal Empire, you see a veiled Muslim woman in a concentration camp uniform and encircled by a halo, which, in Muslim art, is reserved for angels and the Prophet Muhammad alone. She is a woman with a blue face, perhaps a reverence to the Hindu deity of Vishnu, a woman watering plants of what might be the newly born or the unborn. The painting is called *Lilith* (2004) and is a part of a series called *Finding Home*. A religious home is no longer an unbroken identity. Home is as much exile, as the exilic experience is home. Siona's sensibilities toward space recognizes multiple religious and cultural identities. Whatever one thinks of her art, it is as confounding as it is creatively responding to today's realities.

Siona Benjamin's painting illustrates the fact that new challenges have arisen to post-Shoah Jewish–Christian relations. These challenges do not, I suggest, come from people who actively and deliberately contest the theological progress made in Jewish–Christian relations over the last decades, but rather from people who remain largely indifferent to Jewish-Christian dialogue. I am thinking here particularly of younger generations. As I can observe among my students, they seem to take for granted the improved relationships between Jews and Christians, and their interests have shifted to other issues of cultural and religious diversity. They see themselves as spiritual seekers, not as committed to particularity. The relevant literature on religious identity confirms such attitudes and speaks of hybrid religious identities, of hyphenated religious identities, of dual religious belongings, or of multiple religious belongings, and this includes ambiguous religious identifications even within a tradition.[9] These contemporary phenomena have led to a general decline of interest in the particularity of Jewish-Christian dialogue. Also, since the events of 9/11, focus has shifted to Muslim-Christian and Muslim-Jewish dialogue and, more generally, to conversations with the Asian religious traditions. When my religious studies colleagues Karla Suomala, Katharina von Kellenbach, and I convened a four-week international research seminar in 2011 on the intersection of religious pluralism and Jewish-Christian dialogue, we were quite aware of these trends.[10]

Describing themselves not as religious but spiritual, my students seek paths outside of the biblical promise of a covenantal relation. But even when they remain within the Christian or Jewish faith traditions, theological discussions remain, for them, largely foreign and alien. When it comes to the Holocaust, which has been, and will foreseeably remain, a popular topic among students, this event no longer raises questions about religious belonging or challenges them to think theologically. Rather, the Holocaust is of interest to them as a historical event with political and ethical implications concerning tolerance and diversity; it is not an event that compels them to reconfigure Jewish–Christian relations, as it did for the churches right after 1945. Of course, there are a number of other current challenges to post-Shoah Jewish–Christian dialogue, such as new alliances between conservative evangelical groups and activist, militant movements in Israel, such as the Gush Emunim. Or, if we were to sketch the broadest of reasons for the fading interest in Jewish–Christian relations, I could name a number of global anxieties—such as the environmental crisis—that are not sufficiently addressed in the Jewish-Christian dialogue community. The established discourse of post-1945 Jewish-Christian dialogue groups is perceived—and, in my view, to some extent correctly—as circling around a set of worn issues that newcomers, and particularly the younger generation, find somewhat obscure and immaterial to their lives.

But rather than lamenting such a decline in interest, I want to suggest that here lies an opportunity for future Jewish-Christian dialogue if we were willing to apply the processes and lessons we have learned from our particular engagement since 1945 to the current situation. In the wake of the Shoah, Christians and Jews have worked diligently to establish mutual trust and open dialogue and have moved to an acceptance of a covenantal relationship of equals. This did not come easy. It was often a thorny, unsettling, discomforting, painful, and at times upsetting process. And it is this post-Shoah dialogical process, I argue, that can be seen as a gift that Jews and Christians can bring to other communities that experience social tension and religious conflict. It would require, however, to opening up of the established patterns of Jewish–Christian relations to changes. This might be frightening to some, but I think we can do so with some confidence. Christians and Jews, who know themselves in a covenantal relationship to God and to their fellow human beings, a relationship made out of free choice, can embrace the present and future as a not-yet determined reality that constantly draws us into greater intensity and greater complexity of an ever-evolving creation. In other words, we should not fear but embrace change as an opportunity. As Rabbi Joshua

Heschel so pointedly stated in his famous "No Religion Is an Island" speech of 1966: "Parochialism has become untenable. The religions of the world are no more self-sufficient, no more independent, no more isolated than individuals and nations. Horizons are wider, dangers are greater. We are all involved with one another. No religion is an island."[11]

This is where the art of dialogue enters. What does it take for dialogue to be transformative? Clearly, it must transcend the mere exchange of niceties. If we recall that the starting point of the current status of relations between Christians and Jews was the Nazi assault on covenantal relations, then we must realize that effective dialogue begins where it matters, and where it matters, it might hurt, and where it hurts, it leads (when carefully managed) to transformation (Fig. 2).

The kind of dialogical work I have been engaged in for many years goes beyond mere conversation. It goes beyond some of the classic models that are limited to discerning commonalities between people estranged from each other and beyond a mere acknowledging of differences. Instead, the dialogical work I have in mind aims at facilitating and implementing restorative and reconciliatory practices among and

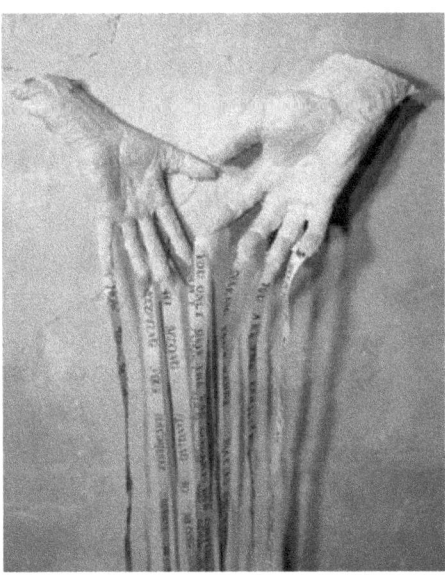

Figure 2. Detail of *Tikkun/Mending* (2006). Baldner and Krondorfer. Paper-sculpture (approx. 60" × 25").

between groups that find themselves in tension and in conflict with each other.

The essential components of the art of dialogue can be grouped into three categories, and I will explain each in some more detail. Effective dialogue needs

1. Memory Work,
2. Reconciliatory Processes, and
3. Restorative Vision

Memory Work

We all have dreams. Some we forget, others we remember. Some we are ashamed to share publicly, others we are eager to talk about. To understand dreams, we need to recall them, acknowledge them, and interpret them. We can call this dream interpretation or dream work. What is true for dreams, I suggest, is in analogical fashion true for memories. We all have them, but to understand them, we need to recall, acknowledge, share, and interpret them.

In situations of communal conflicts that stretch over generations, memory work is particularly important, but also particularly difficult, because memory motivates us to act in particular ways in the present. Unchallenged, memory can serve to fortify our communal borders, defend our social identities, make us cling to stories of suffering and victimization, or insist that we must replay a hero's tale about the past. In contrast to simply *having* memories that get reiterated in families and communities, *memory work* is the attempt to work through troublesome memories and to work toward a place in which we are no longer prisoners of the past but freed to relate anew to people like us and people not like us.

Memory work is not cost-free, especially when we talk about collectively experienced trauma and collectively enacted wrongdoing, as in the Shoah. Judith Lewis Herman writes that "remembering and telling the truth about terrible events are prerequisites both for the restoration of the social order and for the healing of individual victims."[12] Healing individual pain and restoring social order are two essential elements for mending the world affected by the Holocaust—this twentieth-century event that still informs our understanding of today's ethnic, religious, state-sponsored, and genocidal conflicts around the globe. Searching for responses to the history and memory of the Holocaust, hence, is neither a private obsession nor a nostalgic task, but a necessity for the future.

The Abrahamic religions know that we do not remember simply for the sake of memory. Rather, memory infuses and informs the present. Edward Kessler writes that such dialogue needs "a renewed emphasis on *memoria futuri*," the positive aspects of memory. "Religious remembrance," he writes, "is not an act of nostalgia, but one that empowers the present."[13] In the Abrahamic traditions, the past presence has always been important. For Jews, Muslims, and Christians, memory is not just an accumulation of historical facts but a pillar of spirituality, a source of revelation, and a mechanism by which people can take account of their moral selves. When Christians, for example, celebrate the Communion (or the Eucharist), they celebrate the remembrance of the presentness of Jesus Christ in the midst of their community. "This is my body …. Do this in remembrance of me." When Muslims pray five times a day, or fast during the annual month of Ramadhan, or do the *hajj* once in a lifetime, they engage in acts of remembrance. Theologically, this is known as the concept of *dhikr*—Arabic for remembrance, a reminder, an evocation. The opposite of *dhikr* is forgetfulness, and forgetfulness leads Muslim believers astray from the path with and to God. When Jews remember the Exodus during the annual Passover seder, or remember the first attempted mass killing of Jews during Purim, or when they remember the destruction of the Temple at Tisha b'Av or God's mercy during Yom Kippur, they too emphasize that memory makes spiritual demands on believers in the present. In short, the religious act of remembrance is more than a mere commemoration of a historical event. It is the acknowledgment of a past whose presence must be actualized now and in the future. Interreligious dialogue, then, is in a good position to bring awareness to the necessary task of memory work for groups living in the aftermath of traumatic memory and in continuous social conflict.

However, memory work, whether done with or without a commitment to a particular faith, does not come easy. When Christians and Jews, or Germans and Jews, or any other social group in conflict enter into transformative dialogue, questions of group identity and loyalty are raised. One's sense of belonging may become unsettled. Memory work brings up defensiveness, fears of betrayal, and a desire to withdraw into protected and familiar mental territory. Memory work, hence, needs guidance. For when it works well, it compels us to reconsider our assumptions and renders us vulnerable in the presence of the other, which is an indispensable seed for any personal and social transformation to happen (Fig. 3).

Memory work is arduous because it is channeled through the dynamics of blame and shame, anger and guilt—dynamics that affect individuals so profoundly precisely because these are not just personal but transindividual problems anchored in our cultures. I have seen this in encounters between young Germans and American Jews; among my students of Hispanic, black, white, and migrant backgrounds during racial reconciliation seminars; among Palestinian and Israeli educators in peace training sessions; or among German clergy and rabbis from the Chicago area when we commemorated together the dead at a liturgical moment in the former concentration camp of Buchenwald.

Similar dynamics have also been palpable at every step in the work of the Jewish German Dance Theatre, the performance group of Jewish American dancers and non-Jewish German actors, which Lisa Green Cudek and I co-founded in the 1980s.[14] The same dynamics left their mark on the many post-performance discussions with German audiences when we toured Germany in 1988 and 1989. Working through memory is a force also present in just about every piece that Karen Baldner and I have created in our ongoing dialogue. She and I searched for a visual lan-

Figure 3. *Connection* (2002). Pencil on paper. Student Kamila Nevludova drew this in response to a dialogue program on the Holocaust.

guage that preserves the intensity and intimacy of sharing with each other our Jewish and German family roots that are so deeply embedded in the very tangible landscape of Europe (Fig. 4).

Reconciliatory Processes

If memory work is an important element in the art to dialoguing, I want to stress again that it is not an exercise for the sake of memory itself. The art of dialogue does not consist in storing, archiving, and displaying the past—this is the task of historians and museums—but in affecting positively social relationships in the present.

After the Holocaust, it was certainly not easy for Christians to trace and acknowledge the patristic beginnings of the teachings of contempt (of Jews), or to confront themselves with the forced medieval disputations that often ended with the expulsion of the Jewish conversation partners, or to acknowledge the torturous and lethal proceedings of the Spanish Inquisition of suspected *marranos* (Jewish converts to Christianity who secretly practiced Judaism). To return to these troubled times was not meant to re-inscribe what was already known historically but to change and transform contemporary relationships. The goal of memory work is not to fortify entrenched communal identities, but to soften these bor-

Figure 4. *For now we see in a mirror, dimly, but then we will see face to face* (2012). Krondorfer (installation with map, window panels, photoprint, horsehair).

ders, move into territory of unsettling empathy, and risk a transformed understanding of each other. Memory work, in other words, is embedded in the framework of reconciliatory processes.

For a reconciliatory process to work, the results cannot be predetermined. Reconciliation might happen, but it can never be forced. Also, reconciliation is not the same as forgiveness. It does not even require forgiveness, a fact that is often misunderstood. Reconciliation is a regaining of trust, of trusting relationships; just as relationships are always open to change, reconciliatory processes are open-ended. They simply ask participating parties to share their experiences, ideas, fears, and concerns in direct and honest ways in the presence of the other. Reconciliatory processes encourage the engaged parties to show respect but not politeness. Importantly, in reconciliatory processes, one learns to empathize (although not necessarily agree with) the experiences of the other. Such empathetic identification, however temporary, is unsettling and therefore initially resisted.

There are no magic bullets in these processes. We are not talking miracles or divine intervention, and religiously grounded Christians and Jews can understand this easily. Knowing themselves enfolded in and bound to a covenantal relationship, they understand that success is not measured by quantity or by perfect end results but by one's willingness to walk a righteous path. It is like the Talmudic story where a student of Torah is about to give up when confronted with the seemingly impossible task of removing a huge heap of dust, because it would take a lifetime to do so. But the sage advices him that it is "not incumbent upon thee" to remove it all, just to remove a small part every day.[15]

For example, in 2010, I facilitated a weeklong intensive seminar for a group of fifty Jewish Israelis, Muslim Palestinians, and secular Germans in Beit Jalah, the West Banks, based on the principles outlined above. Sometimes, when people hear me talk about these encounters, they ask with a skeptical voice, "and…did it bring peace to the Middle East?" Of course, it did not. Evidence of transformative change does not lie in miracles, but in small signs, such as the exchange of a brief gesture between a Palestinian young man from Ramallah, who had been angry and spouting politicized phrases for much of the time, and an orthodox young woman from the suburbs of Tel Aviv, who never had met Palestinians before on a personal level. As both of these young people were standing in line for lunch, they exchanged a friendly poke with their elbows and smiled at each other. If success were measured by standards of grand political solutions, such dialogical encounters would be disappointing. No peace agreement descended upon this troubled territory after our meeting at Beit Jalah. And yet, such a gesture captures the effectiveness of creating dialogical frames in intractable situations: The little poke with the elbow (with no further words exchanged) was all that these two people were able to muster at the time. Amidst cultivated mistrust and political hatred, it signaled the possibility of a different symbolic order (Fig. 5).

Restorative Vision

Memory work and reconciliatory processes need to be guided by a restorative vision, the third element of the art of dialogue. Theology may speak in this situation the language of eschatology, of mending, or of messianic hopes, although, of course, quite distinctly in the Jewish and Christian communities. There are also non-theological terms that I find extraordinarily helpful when articulating such a vision, like social repair, restorative justice, moral repair, or the moral imagination. They help to envision alternatives to violent, unjust, and discriminatory social and political systems.

Figure 5. Memory work with Palestinian and Israeli participants (2009). Left: Israeli sculpture; right: Palestinian sculpture.

Crucial for any restorative vision is a commitment to fairness and justice; otherwise, desired solutions may just be reduced to apologetic and exculpatory mechanisms in which legal immunity or political amnesty safeguard perpetrators while disempowering victimized communities. A restorative vision needs to live with the *as if*, the not-yet fulfilled promise, always falling short of what one ultimately knows to be right and fair. It is like the fuel that keeps a dialogue running; it is a guide assisting through times of frustration, when patience runs thin in dialogical encounters. A restorative vision leads participating parties in the right direction even as they may feel, at times, dissatisfied by compromises or derailed by the many detours that it takes.

For me, a restorative vision must be grounded in responsiveness to the other. Caring responsiveness asks for such things I mentioned earlier: openness, honesty, respect, vulnerability in the presence of the other, unsettling empathy, self-awareness. I call such responsiveness to the other an ethics of relationality. Relationality enables us to appreciate and support the dialogical work that is required when approaching diversity and differences with the aim of moving beyond entrenched positions and toward restored relations.

To speak about responsiveness to others in a world of religious and cultural diversity is not just empty rhetoric, because such dialogical responsiveness obligates us. Often, this obligation is not simply a matter of personal choice, but one of historical contingency. I can say with certainty that the Holocaust, for someone born and raised in Germany, is of importance because I find myself embedded in historical and social conditions that have been passed on to me through national and family origins. Whatever I wish to think or do as an individual, it does not remove me from the fact that in 1943, for example, my father, at the age of 17, spent almost a year in an antiaircraft platoon of the German army, only two miles away from a Jewish slave labor camp in Poland. These stories, these conditions, reach deeper and beyond my individuality; they determine some of the choices I can make as a human being called into freedom (Fig. 6).

Today, I find myself engaged in a web of multiple relationships with Jews, Germans, Poles, Christians, Americans, and more recently Palestinians, but also in relational webs determined by my gender, parenthood, religion, race, and professional affiliation. These relation-

Figure 6. Detail. *pushmepullyou* (2007). Baldner and Krondorfer. The page shows linocut and reads: "Blechhammer 1943–44."

ships cannot be fully understood if I presented myself, or if I were perceived by others, in and through only *one* identity: I am not just a German, I am not just a Christian, I am not just the son of my father, and I am not just a scholar of religious studies. I am all of these, but also always more than the sum total of these aspects. Unless the sum total of these multiple sources of identification and experiences are integrated in those places where my life intersects with the lives of others, neither I nor my conversation partners can grow and mature.

Does my commitment to the Shoah limit me as I seek to engage reconciliatory mechanisms in contemporary conflicts that plague the globe? It is a question I often ask myself. I have struggled with it and have come to the ethical position of "responsiveness to the other." Let me explain.

Because I inhabit a special relation to the victims and the perpetrators of the Shoah and to the communities to which they belong, I can safely speak of the singular significance that the Holocaust holds for me as for many others in the Jewish-Christian dialogue community. Because the Shoah is of utmost relevance to us, we do not need to expect from others to give it the same weight and significance. In places where the Holocaust intersects or overlaps with other burdens of past or present systems of injustice, the value of dialogical responsiveness dictates new and innovative forms of bringing into play the history and memory of the Holocaust. For example, I cannot easily share the singularity that the Holocaust has for me when I am working in a global context, either with

Palestinians and Israelis, on transitional justice in South Africa, or with students in racial reconciliation retreats. In diverse cultural contexts, it will do me no good to insist on the uniqueness of the Shoah when today's world is ripped apart by multiple violent conflicts or to insist on the uniqueness of Jewish-Christian dialogue while living in a society that is religiously diverse, mixed, and complex.

When engaged in global conflict solutions in a religiously and culturally diverse world, we are asked to become conscious of dialogical relationality. This does not imply, however, that we should expect from our conversation partners that they give equal weight to the faith, beliefs, and values that are dear to us. Each of us is called into the responsibility of his or her own historical contingency. In conversations with African Americans, for example, I can bring the significance that the Holocaust has for me into the conversation without expecting this to change the meaning that slavery holds for my dialogue partners. In encounters with Palestinians, I can testify to the kind of responsibility I have toward Jewish Israelis because of my link to the Holocaust without having to expect that Palestinians will share my view or that, therefore, the value of the Naqba is diminished. Conversely, I can expect from my conversation partners that they too do not insist on their particular ethnic, national, or religious narratives, but that they are responsive also to my narrative and experiences. In other words, if we want to engage the meaning and place of our values, religious beliefs, and practices, we must proceed together in mutual recognition of our shared responsiveness to each other. It cannot happen one-sidedly. It is mutual responsiveness that leads to transformation.

The art of dialogue calls us into a caring responsiveness to the other within a framework of memory work, reconciliatory processes, and a vision of restorative justice. As much as we wish, we cannot predict the outcome of such dialogue, because it always takes a risk to act compassionately toward the one we do not know yet. What the art of dialogue insists on, though, is to train our moral imagination and empathy, however unsettling this can be. As human beings, as moral agents, we have the capacity to transcend the limitations of merely self-interested action and we can, instead, move toward other-directed care. When we see the face of the other, we might see a troubled past, but we must also look into the present face of the other to see the possibilities of our future relationships.

Notes

1. This text is a slightly edited and revised version of the *Jerome S. Cardin Memorial Lecture*, presented at Loyola University, Baltimore, on March 25, 2012.
2. "Witnessing and Re-Imagining Through the Arts: Meditation on a Dialogical Process," Björn Krondorfer (in collaboration with Karen Baldner), *CrossCurrents* (December 2010):495–514.
3. Sherman, Franklin (ed.), *Bridges: Documents of the Christian-Jewish Dialogue: Volume One: The Road to Reconciliation (1945–1985)* (New York: Paulist Press, 2011), p. xiii. See also Yaakov Ariel, "Interfaith Dialogue and the Golden Age of Christian-Jewish Relations," *Studies in Christian-Jewish Relations* 6 (2011):Ariel CP 1-18 (http://ejournals.bc.edu/ojs/index.php/scjr).
4. *Bridges*, p. xiii.
5. Ibid., p. xvi.
6. Ibid, p. xiv.
7. The Christian Scholars Group on Christian–Jewish Relations published, for example, *Seeing Judaism Anew: Christianity's Sacred Obligation*, ed. Mary C. Boys (Lanham: Sheed & Ward, 2005).
8. For an image of "Relatum-Silence," see Dawn-Michelle Baude, "Encounters Between Seer and Seen: Lee Ufan at the Guggenheim," in *artcritical: the online magazine of art and ideas* (www.artcritical.com/2011/09/13/lee-ufan/), accessed May 2012. The image sites of search engines like google or bing also bring up a number of pictures of this installation.
9. For example, Cornille, Catherine, *The Impossibility of Interreligious Dialogue* (New York: Herder & Herder, 2008); ibid. and Christopher Conway (ed.), *Interreligious Hermeneutics* (Eugene, OR: Wipf and Stock, 2010); Rita M. Gross, "Buddhism and Religious Diversity," *Tricycle* (Fall 2011):n.p. (www.tricycle.com/feature/buddhism-and-religious-diversity?page=0,0).
10. "Explorations at the Intersection of Religious Pluralism and Jewish-Christian Dialogue," Research Coolidge Colloquium 2011, hosted at Union Theological Seminary and Auburn Theological Seminary, New York City.
11. "No Religion Is an Island" was first printed in 1966 in *Union Seminary Quarterly Review* and is reprinted as Document 68 in *Bridges* by Franklin Sherman, pp. 419–436, 421.
12. Lewis Herman, Judith, *Trauma and Recovery: The Aftermath of Violence-From Domestic Abuse to Political Terror* (New York: Basic Books, 1992), p. 1.
13. Kessler, Edward, *Introduction to Jewish-Christian Relations* (Cambridge: Cambridge University Press, 2010), p. 201.
14. See Krondorfer, *Remembrance and Reconciliation: Encounters Between Young Jews and Germans* (New Haven, CT: Yale University Press, 1995).
15. See Polano, H., *The Talmud: Selections* (London: Frederick Warne & Co, 1877), p. 245.

CROSSCURRENTS

A DIFFERENT KIND OF DIALOGUE?
Messianic Judaism and Jewish-Christian Relations

Yaakov Ariel

In the 1970s, both Jews and Christians were surprised to see the rise of a vigorous movement of Christian Jews. Messianic Jews embraced the evangelical definition of Christians as people who undergo experiences of conversion or being born again, as well as evangelical manners of reading the Bible and evangelical codes of personal morality, but wished to maintain a measure of Jewish culture and identity. The same years were the heydays of Christian-Jewish dialogue, which brought about a breakthrough in the relationship between the two faiths. Situated in a very different cultural and theological climate, Messianic Jews have engaged in a very different experiment in Christian-Jewish relations that also signified a new understanding of the relationship between the two faiths, albeit in a very different manner than liberal Christians and Jews envisioned. Students of Christian-Jewish relations in our time should therefore pay attention to the Messianic Jewish movement, which, like the dialogue, also signified a change of heart in relation to the Jews, this time among conservative Christians.

Historical background and early years

The roots of the new movement can be traced to Pietist and evangelical missionary ideology in the modern era that advocated the position that accepting the Christian faith did not stand in contradiction to Jewish identity but rather made it more complete. The evangelical premillennialist view that has considered the Jews to be the Chosen People has also served to offer justification for maintaining Jewish identity, customs, and symbols. There were attempts at creating communities of Jewish-Christians in the nineteenth century, but such experiments were short-lived. "Judaizing" had traditionally been considered heresy, and many expressed suspicion toward the idea of separate Jewish congregations. Converts too were often afraid of arousing suspicion that their conversions were not genuine and, as a rule, chose to join non-Jewish churches.[1] Attitudes gradually changed, and in the 1920s, the Presbyterian Church, USA, initiated the establishment of Jewish-Christian congregations, intending them to serve as centers of evangelism among the Jews as well as communities where being ethnically Jewish was normative.

The more assertive and independent movement of Messianic Judaism that came on the scene in the 1970s represented a new generation that possessed unprecedented freedoms of choice, including the amalgamation of traditions, which previous generations had considered alien to each other. This offered Messianic Jews a sense of mission as they felt that they were healing historical injuries. The new movement has attempted to create a young and exciting vision of Christianity that worked around traditional views of a faith alien to Jews. Evangelical Christian attitudes also changed and became more accepting toward ethnic pride and incorporation of symbols and customs from other traditions, such as Native Americans, although an amalgamation of the Christian faith and Jewish identity was, perhaps, even more daring. The war in June 1967, between Israel and its neighbors, also affected the manner in which evangelical Christians had come to view the Jews and their role in history, boosting the converts' status, their pride in their roots, and their desire to maintain Jewish identity.[2]

In the first phase of the movement, Jewish converts to Christianity established congregations on their own initiative, which were largely independent of the control of missionary societies or Christian denominations. An early and central congregation, within the larger movement, has been Beth Yeshua in Philadelphia. In the late 1960s, Joe Finkelstein, a chemist and a Jewish convert to Christianity, gathered a group of Jewish teenagers who were looking for an alternative to their parents' middle-class environment, as well as a haven from the more dangerous aspects of the counterculture. The Christian-Jewish communities demanded abstinence from drugs, alcohol, and premarital sex and encouraged their members to obey the law and work hard toward careers. Finkelstein initially brought the new converts to the Presbyterian-sponsored Hebrew

Christian center in downtown Philadelphia, but the young converts did not take well to the older Jewish-Presbyterian congregation, viewing it as lacking in Jewish atmosphere, and they decided to establish their own congregation, which grew considerably.[3] Messianic congregations serve as centers of evangelism with sermons promoting the Christian evangelical creed, striving to inspire the non-converted in the audience to convert.

Christian and Jewish reactions

While Messianic Judaism represented Christian evangelical theology and morality, it struggled in its early years to secure its legitimacy within the larger evangelical movement, on the whole very successfully. One of its defenders, James Hutchens, wrote his doctoral dissertation "A Case for Messianic Judaism" at the evangelical Fuller Theological Seminary in 1974. Hutchens, who converted to Judaism while holding on to his belief in the Messiahship of Jesus, advocated Messianic Judaism as a means for Jews to accept the Christian faith while retaining the cultural components of their Jewish heritage. Beyond "the core faith," the cultural dresses were variable and open for choice, he contended.[4] Attempting to advance the cause of evangelism among Jews, missionary groups, such as the American Board of Missions to the Jews, and denominations, such as the Assemblies of God, began sponsoring Messianic congregations, often more moderate in inserting elements of the Jewish tradition. In a manner typical to many ethnic evangelical communities, a number of Messianic Jewish communities share buildings with non-Jewish congregations, signifying the affinity in faith. It was, perhaps, not a coincidence that when the evangelical group, the Promise Keepers, launched a major rally in Washington, D.C., in 1997, two groups of born-again Christians were particularly visible. Messianic Jews came to the gathering dressed with *talitot*, prayer shawls, and holding *shofarot* and rams horns, and Native Americans came dressed in their traditional attire and decorated with American Indian symbols.

Liberal Protestants have looked less favorably upon the new movement than their conservative counterparts. The years in which Messianic Judaism made its debut were the heyday of the Jewish-Christian Dialogue. From the liberal point of view, there was no necessity any more for Jews to turn to Christianity, certainly not to conservative forms of Christianity, which liberals cared little for anyhow.[5] The liberals were interested in speaking with "real" Jews, and in learning from a "sister religion," not from Messianic Judaism, which they did not consider to be a valid form of the religion they were now looking at in a new light. Both liberal Christians and Jews considered Messianic Judaism to be a bizarre fringe group and did not take it very seriously. And those engaged in dialogue were well aware of the negative reaction of Jews to all forms of evangelism and their concern over Jewish continuity.

While not unified or consistent, Jewish reactions to the new movement demonstrated what Jews considered the legitimate boundaries of Judaism as a religion and as a community. In general, Jews did not take seriously the Messianic Jewish belief that one could embrace Christianity and remain Jewish and considered the groups to be either fraudulent or bizarre. "Beth Yeshua," wrote Michael Mach about the Messianic Jewish congregation, "is part of...an Orwellian world of Jewish-Christian confusion where things are never as they ought to be, and rarely as they seem...".[6] Rabbi Ronald Gittelsohn wrote "Jews for Jesus is only one of several aberrant religious or psuedoreligious cults flourishing today on the American scene."[7] Jewish Orthodox activists founded organizations to fight groups such as Messianic Jews, whom they considered to be in essence Christian missionaries. In Israel, the ultra-Orthodox organization *Yad L'Achim* (A Hand for the Brethren) has made a name for itself in combating missionaries and congregations of Jewish believers in Jesus.[8] The rise and further spread of Messianic Judaism stirred also liberal Jews to action. In the 1980s, Jewish leaders and organizations thought that they should prepare Jewish youth for a possible encounter with the new rhetoric of Christian evangelism and the option of Messianic Judaism, by publishing "know what to answer" books. These tracts did not speak in one voice, each book representing a different Jewish point of view. Lawrence M. Silverman, a Reform rabbi, demonstrated a progressive Jewish opinion declaring that in contrast to evangelical Christian and Messianic Jewish beliefs "The messianic age will come to pass in this world!" and "We do not believe that personal salvation and eternal life should be overriding concerns in one's life."[9]

While many Jews have continued to look upon Messianic Judaism suspiciously as an alien and bizarre development, some have reconsidered their position. Messianic Judaism grew and has turned into a permanent feature of the religious and cultural scene in Jewish population centers around the globe, and some Jews began looking at them in a new manner.

Articles on Messianic Jews in Jewish periodicals, such as *Moment* and the *Jerusalem Report,* appearing in 1990–2010, treated the converts more respectfully and presented their case in a surprisingly impartial tone. In 2000, Dan Cohn-Sherbok, a Reform rabbi, published a book on Messianic Judaism, which in essence called for an inclusive definition of Judaism and the acceptance of the movement.

A subculture of their own

While struggling to be accepted, Messianic Judaism has, throughout 1970–2010, developed its own subculture, complete with conferences and organizations, youth movements and summer camps, prayer books, hymnals, theological tracts, periodicals, and web sites. By the early 2010s, there were about 300 Messianic Jewish congregations in America with a noticeable presence in evangelical life going beyond those numbers. There are about 100 communities in Israel and dozens more in Europe, Latin America, and the former Soviet bloc. Messianic Jewish communities follow mainstream conservative evangelical social and cultural norms. For example, all Messianic rabbis or ministers are men. However, Messianic Judaism is not a unified or uniform community. A major division between Messianic congregations is between Charismatics and non-Charismatics, reflecting a division within the larger evangelical community. Another difference is over Jewish tradition and rites. On the one end of the spectrum stand those who have been very hesitant to observe Jewish rites and customs and have adopted a liturgy close to that of non-Jewish congregations, and on the other end, those who advocate extensive incorporation of Jewish rites, including reading from a Torah scroll, wearing *yarmulkes* during services, and placing an arc of the covenant in the sanctuary. None, however, have made the claim that there is a requirement to observe Jewish rites in order to be justified in the eyes of God.[10] Many Messianic congregations have compiled or adopted Messianic Jewish *siddurs* (prayer books), which pick and choose elements of the traditional Jewish prayer book, coupled with prayers that give expression to faith in Jesus and his role as the Redeemer. Almost all congregations celebrate Jewish holidays, such as Passover, reading the liturgy from Messianic *Haggadot,* which similarly pick elements of traditional *Haggadot* with prayers that give expression to the members' faith in Jesus.[11]

In spite of their promotion of Jewish identity, symbols and cultural elements, Messianic Jewish communities have attracted non-Jewish members, who often account for a large percentage, and at times the majority, of the participants. The percentage of intermarried couples within the congregations is also high.[12] In essence, Messianic congregations serve as meeting spaces for Jews and non-Jews holding to a conservative Protestant faith as well as to the idea of the role of Jews and Israel in God's plans for humanity.[13] Messianic Jews, like conservative evangelicals in general, subscribe to conservative social and political views, seeing themselves as patriotic Americans or Israelis. Messianic Jews support Israel, along similar understanding as those of many premillennialist evangelicals. Their relation to Israel serves to re-affirm their Jewish identity at the same time that it carries the theological perceptions and political agenda of the evangelical camp.

The Messianic Jewish messages and vocabulary had a dramatic effect in Israel in the last three decades. Previously, the number of conversions to Christianity in Israel was small, but the tide changed. Faith in Zionism as an all-encompassing ideology, providing hope, meaning, and a sense of purpose, weakened considerably, leaving plenty of room for alternative faiths to gain followers in the Israeli spiritual and communal market.[14] Young Israelis began joining new religious movements and thousands became "returnees to tradition," while others accepted the Christian faith in its Messianic Jewish form. The community of Messianic Jews in Israel grew from no more than a few hundred people in the mid-1960s to over 15,000 by the 2010s.[15] Much of the stigma surrounding conversion to Christianity has faded, at least in the non-Orthodox community, as Israeli culture became more inclusive and diverse. For many Israelis, the image of Christianity, particularly in its Western European or American form, has changed dramatically, turning from a hostile faith to the religion of friendly visitors, volunteers, colleagues, friends, and supporters. A public opinion poll in the late 1980s discovered that most Israelis were willing to accept Messianic Jews.[16] This is not to say that Messianic Jews did not encounter opposition and even occasional harassment.

Messianic Jewish theology

Struggling for acceptance as both Jews and Christians, Messianic Jewish thinkers have produced a series of theological tracts that have come to define and defend the movement's unique path. Their work has not been uniform and has given voice to a spectrum of opinions, although almost all thinkers have contended that Jews who have embraced Christianity were following in the path of the original Christians, making Messianic Judaism a continuation of the earliest form of Christianity. David Stern, a leader and thinker in the Messianic Jewish movement in Israel, translated and edited a Messianic Jewish New Testament. In it, he changed the traditional translation of Paul's *Epistle to the Hebrews* into a *Letter to Messianic Jews*.[17] Another trend in Messianic Jewish thinking has been a gradual move into a more independent form of Jewish-Christian identity. This development has manifested itself in the work of Arnold Fruchtenbaum, a relatively moderate Messianic thinker. In the 1970s, Fruchtenbaum defined himself as a Hebrew Christian, a more moderate form of Jewish-Christian identity, and was skeptical about the more assertive forms of Messianic Judaism.[18] In *Hebrew Christianity: Its Theology, History and Philosophy*, Fruchtenbaum declared that "the Hebrew Christian should be a member of the local church along with Gentile believers."[19] Fruchtenbaum modified his views a number of years later, and Ariel Ministries, which he founded and led, has been instrumental in the establishment of a number of Messianic Jewish congregations. In 1985, Fruchtenbaum defended the right of Jewish believers in Jesus to establish congregations and observe Jewish rites if they so wished, as long as they looked upon it as an option and did not consider it a requirement toward salvation.[20] David Stern's *Messianic Jewish Manifesto* has been one of the better known Messianic theological tracts, in which he presented the merits and goals of the movement as he understood them: "By providing a Jewish environment for Messianic faith, Messianic Judaism is useful in evangelizing Jews."[21] And: "It is useful in focusing the Church's attention on the Jewish people."[22] Stern's declaration that Messianic Jews are not half Christian and half Jews, but rather fully Christian and fully Jewish has become a cornerstone of Messianic Jewish self-understanding at the turn of the twenty-first century.

At the turn of the twenty-first century, a number of Messianic Jewish thinkers, on both sides of the Atlantic, have come up with new suggestions as to how to understand and practice a more independent amalgamation of Judaism and Christianity. Gershon Nerel, an Israeli Messianic intellectual, has advocated for a greater reliance on the sacred scriptures.

An ardent premillennialist, Nerel views Israel as fulfilling an important role in God's plans for humanity and criticizes Christians who, in his view, undermine Israel.[23] Tsvi Sadan, editor of *Kivun,* a Messianic Jewish Israeli journal, has militated for an independent understanding of the Jewish faith in Jesus divorced from evangelical conservative theology. Mark Kinzer and Stuart Dauermann are founders and leaders of *Hashivenu* ("Bring us Back," in Hebrew), a group of Messianic Jewish intellectuals who promote a more independent Jewish-Christian culture and thought, including the idea that Jewish-Christians should, at least in certain instances, look for inspiration in Jewish, post-Biblical sources and ignore post-scriptural Christian texts that may no longer be very relevant.[24] Using traditional Jewish language, the group has formulated its agenda: "We seek an authentic expression of Jewish life maintaining substantial continuity with Jewish traditions…It is our conviction that *Hashem* brings Messianic Jews to a richer knowledge of himself through a modern day rediscovery of the paths of our ancestors—*Avodah* (liturgical worship), *Torah* (study of the sacred texts), and *Gemilut Chasadim* (deeds of loving-kindness)." Hashivenu and its circle point to the growing diversity within the larger Messianic Jewish movement, where different communities and individuals have placed greater emphasis on varied components of the Jewish-Christian amalgam. One can also look upon the group as an avant-garde, which wishes to transform Messianic Judaism from a movement that adheres to evangelical theology into one that relies more on Jewish sources, creating a more balanced mixture of the two traditions.

Messianic Judaism has challenged traditional Christian and Jewish understandings of the boundaries between the two faiths on a number of levels. It has certainly offered an alternative to Jewish conversion to and disappearance into Christian society and culture. From its own perspective, it has also created an option of being Jewish and Christian at the same time, with some elements in the movement working on strengthening the Jewish component of the amalgam. Somewhat unwittingly, the movement has also posed a challenge to the dialogue and exchange that has developed between liberal Christians and Jews parallel to the rise of Messianic Judaism. The dialogue has been based on the existence of two separate traditions, which, while endlessly diverse, still held some clear borders. Few were willing to consider the Messianic Jewish movement as a borderline set of communities. For many observers treating Messianic Judaism seriously, it was more Christian than Jewish, a Jewish ethnic version of evangelical Christianity. Even as such, Messianic Judaism should be seen as a different kind of dialogue—a development that signified a new chapter in the relationship of conservative Christians toward Judaism and Jews, showing greater appreciation toward Judaism and its symbols and customs. Ironically, while advocating mostly conservative views on political, social, and cultural issues, this evangelical-Jewish movement is an avant-garde form of post-modern realities, in which individuals and communities exercise their freedom to carry a series of identities and struggle to negotiate between them. Such hybrids have become prevalent in contemporary Christian and Jewish communities, which, since the 1960s, often tended toward innovation and amalgamation of different traditions and practices. One can notice that, for example, in the rise of a large movement of Jewish practitioners of Buddhism, many of whom have not seen a contradiction between their Jewish identity and their Buddhist practices. The rise of Messianic Judaism is still more extraordinary than the coming on the scene of Jewish Buddhists, because Judaism and Buddhism do not share a long history of competition and suspicion. These new movements therefore challenge long-prevailing sensitivities and will continue to do so for quite a while.

Notes

1. Cf. Elias Newman, "Looking Back Twenty Five Years," *The Hebrew Christian Alliance Quarterly*, 25 (1940): 24.
2. Louis Goldberg, *Turbulence Over the Middle East: Israel and the Nations in Confrontation and the Coming Kingdom of Peace on Earth* (Neptune, NJ: Loizeaux Brothers, 1982).
3. Cf. Carol Harris-Shapiro, "Syncretism or Struggle: The Case of Messianic Judaism," a Ph.D. dissertation (Temple University, 1992), 44.
4. James Hutchens, "A Case for Messianic Judaism," Ph. D. Dissertation, Fuller Theological Seminary, 1974.
5. cf. James k. Wellman, *Evangelical vs. Liberal: The Clash of Christian Cultures in the Pacific Northwest* (New York: Oxford University Press, 2008).
6. "Jews for Jesus Is New Freak Group," *Jewish Post and Opinion*, May 14, 1971.
7. Ronald Gittlesohn, "Jews for Jesus: Are They Real?" in Gary D. Eisenberg ed., *Smashing the Idols* (Lanham, MD: Jason Aronson, 1988), 171.
8. On ongoing activities of *Yad L'Achim* cf. www.yadlachimusa.org.il
9. Lawrence Silverman, *What to Say When the Missionary Comes to Your Door* (Plymouth, MA: Plymouth Lodge—B'nai Brith, n.d.).
10. See *Sheelot ve Teshuvot* [in Hebrew] (Rischon Letsion: Hagafen Publishing House, 1986), 17–8; Frequently asked Judaism question about Messianic covenant and love messianic outreach. http://www.teshuvah.com/tomj/index.html March 21, 1995.

11. See, for example, Eric Peter Lipson, *Passover Haggadah, A Messianic Celebration* (San Francisco: JFJ Publications, 1986); Ron Tavalin, *Kol Hesed Messianic Haggadah* (N.P.: Dogwood Press, 1993); Harold A. Sevener, ed. *Passover Haggadah for Biblical Jews and Christians* (Orangeburg, NY: Chosen People Publications, n.d.).
12. Cf. Michael Schiffman, *The Return of the Remnant*, 126, and Sidney Goldstein, "Profile of American Jewry: Insights From the 1990 National Jewish Population Survey," *American Jewish Year Book* (1992): 124–28.
13. On non-Jews versus Jews in Messianic Congregations, see Shoshanah Feher, *Passing Over Easter: Constructing the Boundaries of Messianic Judaism* (Walnut Creek, CA: Altamira Press, 1998).
14. Benjamin Beit-Hallahmi, *Despair and Deliverance: Private Salvation in Contemporary Israel* (Albany: State University of New York Press, 1992).
15. Kai Kjaer-Hansen and Bodil F. Skjott, *Facts and Myths About the Messianic Congregation in Israel, 1998-1999, Mishkan* 30/31 (1999). This special issue examines the demographies of Messianic congregations in Israel in the late 1990s. The authors promoted a conservative estimate of the number of Jewish members in such congregations.
16. "Dahaf Report on Israeli Public Opinion Concerning Messianic Jewish Aliyah," (Jerusalem: David Stern, 1988).
17. David H. Stern, *Jewish New Testament* (Jerusalem: Jewish New Testament Publications, 1990), 295.
18. Arnold G. Fruchtenbaum, *Hebrew Christianity: Its Theology, History and Philosophy* (Grand Rapids, MI: Baker Book House, 1974).
19. Fruchtenbaum, *Hebrew Christianity*, 88.
20. "An Interchange on Hebrew Christian/Messianic Jewish Congregation," Appendix 3, in Arnold G. Fruchtenbaum, *Israelology: The Missing Link in Systematic Theology* (Tustin, CA: Ariel Ministries, 1983), 917–49.
21. David H. Stern, *Messianic Jewish Manifesto* (Jerusalem: Jewish New Testament Publications, 1988).
22. Stern, *Messianic Jewish Manifesto*,12.
23. I am thankful to Gershon Nerel for sharing his thoughts with me. On Nerel's ideas, see Richard Harvey, "A Typology of Messianic Jewish Theology," *Mishkan* 57 (2008), 15–6.
24. The group's website: www.hashivenu.org

CROSSCURRENTS

ENCOUNTERING HABITS OF MIND AT TABLE:
Kashrut, Jews, and Christians

Lisa M. Hess

Sensitive to wounded histories, how do Christians and Jews befriend one another? Many will answer this question quite differently. One person feels an invitation to visit a synagogue, perhaps staying for the community Kiddush cup at the conclusion of Shabbat services. Another will find a budding friendship while working at the local soup kitchen or homeless shelter. Even others will share burdens at work, bumbling into deeper collegiality at the copier and across faith lines in a civic space where distinct voices can find expression. This essay suggests a path of companionship between Jews and Christians begun at table, the informal space(s) of shared meals in public space only reminiscent or suggestive of the formal, liturgical or observant space(s). As such, we will explore some potential concerns whenever Christians and Jews sit down to a table with food laden upon it, namely *kashrut* and the collision of long-conditioned habits of mind across intra- and inter-traditional boundaries. Each section begins with some preliminaries—what *kashrut* is and what *habits of mind* means—before exploring how these shape interactions in settings of table fellowship within and across traditional lines of identity and understanding. What follows is a small portion of an ethnographic study into *kashrut* observance, undertaken both to learn one tradition's specifications determinative of table fellowship and to explore the Christian habits of mind in encounter with such specifications.

What is Kashrut?

Kashrut (variably transliterated *kashruth* and *kashrus*) refers to the Jewish dietary laws, given expression in Torah as well as centuries of halakhic-legal discourse. From this Hebrew term, we get "kosher," meaning "complying with the dietary laws" or "fit for ritual consumption." Asking *what kashrut is*, however, requires expansive imagination and focused precision. Expansive imagination because Jews of widely varying observance can all be said to be "keeping kosher" even as they observe it quite differently. Kosher means many things to just as many people. Only a focused precision will allow a concrete understanding of what communal and/or ritual practices constitute *kashrut* in any given setting.

Let us start with an image. *Kashrut* is not unlike a plumb line stretched by the sages of rabbinic Judaism between the sacred and mundane, the timeless and finite. It marks a boundary with which to dance or wrestle, whether one desires it to be there or not, whether one identifies with the boundary's originators—that is, Torah, rabbinic Judaism, pious stringencies—or not. In this sense, *kashrut* is an ancient set of obligations (*mitzvot*), a practice of attentiveness or separation, and a way of eating and attending to all matters with respect to food while sensitized to what is defined as sacred, set apart. Traditional definitions of *kashrut* point to texts in Deuteronomy 14 and Leviticus 11, the prohibitions against eating certain animals, against consuming blood of any kind, and against mixing meat and milk. Several contemporary resources are available to pursue the logistics of contemporary observance in Torah interpretation.[1] This study asked nineteen identified/identifiable Orthodox[2] Jews who had shared in table fellowship with me to engage in conversations leading to a more nuanced understanding of what *kashrut* is. What emerged was an understanding of *kashrut* as a path of belonging, a path of differentiation, and ultimately, an intimate wisdom and site of struggle for people with a tradition, a heritage, and a vocation (accepted or resisted) to be a blessing to others.

They were eight women and eleven men. Fourteen live in metropolitan New York City (NYC), one in Denver, and four in southwestern Ohio. Four grew up in midwestern cities, fourteen in metropolitan NYC and/or Eastern Seaboard cities (NYC, NJ, CT, PA), and one in Israel. They demonstrated a high value of professions, learning, and family traditioning.[3] Lived commitment to an historic tradition was shared by all, though expressed quite variously. All were critically reflective in a deliberative, coherent way about their received heritage. My own role was one of a Christian outsider who had been invited into table fellowship, though one participant was once removed (i.e., connection occurred through a companionship begun in table fellowship).[4] As such, I was a listening companion, with a sense of surprise, curiosity, and gratitude.

For many, if not most of the study, *kashrut* is a path of belonging. It is not individually crafted or negotiable, except within the ongoing argument between texts and community. One's observance is determined by the community in which one belongs. This observance need not be particularly sacred, as popularly understood, attested by several atheists in the study. For some, of course, *kashrut* is an intimately sacred pact with the Holy One of Israel, Hashem. It is enacted allegiance that says "I love you" to the G!d[5] of Abraham, Isaac, and Jacob from one who has been chosen for such observance. More often than not, however, *kashrut* seems to signal relationships within family and into networks of close-knit community. It demonstrates accountability within a loose but definable web of belonging.

Simultaneously, *kashrut* serves as a means of differentiating from family, at least for this generation. Many participants' parents, sensitized to Jewish identity and isolation in post-Holocaust years, chose to emphasize American or civic identities. One participant did not find out about her Jewish identity until she was 24, at her grandmother's funeral. *Kashrut* offers her a path of consistency and integrity and affirmation of what had been hidden for so long. Another lived in Manhattan but his parents emphatically did *not* observe. Naturally, as he left home for college and then married, he chose to observe, eventually selecting Orthodox observance to shape his own children's Jewishness. As generational tides would have it, of course, all four children do not observe his way of *kashrut* though strongly identify as Jewish. For each of these participants, however, observing *kashrut* was the means to heighten Jewish identity while differentiating from one's parents.

For good, for G!d, for ill, *kashrut* appears to be an intensely intimate wisdom and site of struggle of a people and the individuals within such a people. It offers belonging, a coherent sense of repeatedly chosen identity, and a regular sense of relationship to something or someone greater than oneself. One participant has wrestled with *kashrut* all his life, though I suspect he would not know who he was without it. Another articulated ultra-orthodox observance as the liberation of mind. His observance is so concrete, so unquestionable, that he can think in perceivedly "unorthodox" fashion without fear of intra-traditional reprisal. For another, his observance accompanies him throughout the day—*kashrut*, blessings spoken and unspoken—as he comes home in devotion to his non-Jewish spouse. The observance provides unending opportunities for him to enact his Jewishness amidst a complex web of Jew and non-Jew relations. Shared intra-traditionally, within Jewish communities, I overheard *kashrut* as a potential weapon of tribal exclusion, an unending ladder to human perfection, and a fence of identity maintaining a militant separation between insiders and outsiders.

In the end, we return to the plumb line. Regardless of whether one is close to it by inheritance or choice, "kosher" and "Jewish" are minimally, popularly associated—whether by intention of the observant or presumption of outsiders. From those who observe, in this study, I understand *kashrut* to offer to some a precious opportunity, to others an intermittent burden, while for others it can mean an unreflective custom while living into human fullness, sharpening teeth of identity against the irrepressible wisdom of the Sages, whether they like it or not. The significance of mutual understandings deepens because we are all—Jew and non-Jew alike—faced with this plumb line. Today's food industries show marked increase in kosher supervision (see *Kosher Nation*), quite independent from proscribed religious rationales.[6] When "kosher" comes up in civic conversation, it is a cultural meme connecting Jewishness and eating restrictions. People assume all Jews keep kosher, or should. Popular conception demonstrates a (mis)understanding of what *kashrut* is, captive to the law, a legalism with little freedom or value for living in faith.

So when Christians and Jews approach any table with food, what collision of attitudes and habits of mind might we anticipate, even steward with hope for new ways of companioning across differences? To find out, I decided to listen to the ways in which *kashrut* is perceived, experienced within, and shaped by Christian understandings of scriptural authority and practices. What habits of mind are outsiders bringing—in my case, various strands of Christians who hold to scriptural authority—to the Jewish observance of *kashrut* ever more common in our public spaces?

Habits of mind for (potential) stewardship of table fellowship

The question of *Christian* habits of mind in encounter with *kashrut* emerged when stewarding a worship event co-led by a Modern Orthodox rabbi at a Midwestern seminary. Though the phrase *habits of mind* has curricular connotations within educational circles (i.e., the work of Art Costa and Bena Kallick),[7] I intend it to refer to the *received and discerned attitudes, thoughts, vocabulary and categories brought in critical reflection upon a communal situation or practice*. In a multipurpose space of worship and of common meals, my rabbinic friend and I were forced to navigate around the centrality of the Eucharistic table in the Christian community, the sharing of Shabbat table practices within an educational setting, and the various food-specific options necessary to share table fellowship. In the process, I became aware of a multitude of actions I "saw" with my *own* liturgical tradition's interpretations, while the rabbi was bringing his tradition's Orthodox observance into the shared event. What attitudes, thoughts, vocabulary, and categories were shaping my Christian outsider understanding of another tradition's expressions? How might I describe them, attentive but not limited to textual traditions and definitions? To answer these questions, during the season of Lent 2011, my husband and I spent four weeks maintaining a kosher home before being released from the practice to study Paul's *Letter to the Galatians*. I was both surprised and bemused to encounter startling habits of mind for a theological academic committed to interreligious learning or "learning in the presence of an other."[8] I discovered unbidden polemics, presumptions, and an impolitic misunderstanding of this potential wisdom way of honoring life called *kashrut*.

The four weeks of keeping kosher at home were intended to learn more about the practiced reality of *kashrut* observance, but more importantly, to feel/learn what it was like to surrender to (or have imposed) Jewish norms in the private Christian space of our home, our table, and our kitchen. Historically, of course, it has been the reverse—Christian norms imposed upon Jewish community(ies) in public spaces. "Being released from the practice" meant to imitate the presumed "freedom from the Law" popularly espoused by Paul in his *Letter to the Galatians*. The whole point was to encounter and observe as a Christian outsider and then to describe any habits of mind arising.

When I attempted to observe with the rigor required for Orthodox observance,[9] I discovered an internalized compulsion within me, accompanied by an unsightly rage at "their" overwhelming expectation. This compulsion originated in my own family, of course, with its disposition toward over-achievement. The unsightly rage erupted much less from "their law" and much more from long-forgotten experiences of exclusion and fears of isolation. A crack in an unconscious polemic about "their law" had begun. Without much self-judgment, I noted these attitudes and attempted to describe them as they arose. Rigorous discipline in the observance I *could* maintain then offered its fruits. I knew a previously unknown, sensate interconnectedness of both mundane and transcendent. I felt a glimmer of the holiness of this observance, what I would call a "practice" and grew to love its structured holiness in my life. I began to know a life in the law I had been told was not there, not accessible to a confessing Christian disciple.

Then at an interfaith seder at the local university, I found myself uncontrollably assessing the rigor of *kashrut* observance of the hosting Jewish leaders and "their" event. I was horrified to discover a ravenous self-righteousness in my own mind. I had unknowingly received the passion of a convert to observance, with enough fire to do damage in *two* traditions. Watching my mind go through its new paces, I smiled sadly, keeping my mouth shut. Comments from a couple of Jewish companions began to make sense to me—how *kashrut* can be used as a weapon of tribal exclusion and how it can injure internal community interactions across difference. But then it was time to relinquish the observance and receive my own Christian freedom at home again. I was relieved *and* I grieved terribly. Normalcy of Christian "freedom" from Jewish dietary laws returned, but was experienced as loss. I looked to Paul's letter, a familiar text in my own Christian formation, and it felt foreign. I could no longer withstand Paul's polemic about "the law." I knew a life in the law deep in my own bones, from my own experience of observance.

Without treading into assumed scriptural expertise—I am not a biblical scholar—I have been returned to my own sacred scripture with new eyes, seeing interpretive assumptions and practices that have prevented or inhibited shared table fellowship between Christians and Jews. A lifelong Presbyterian of open-hearted inclinations, I had yet inherited an implicit sense of Jewish dietary laws as a matter of restrictions alone, an imposition and exclusion of outsiders from an insider legalism. When Paul asked, "Why then the law?" in chapter 3 of Galatians, I was primed to interpret everything to come in terms of law and gospel, "their" legalism and "our" freedom.

After the kosher experiment, however, I found myself resistant to Paul's polemical tone and purpose. Concerns of a newly forming ecclesial community such as the one in Galatia will always be impassioned, fervent, and either uncertain or overly certain. Differentiation from previous norms in other sociocultural or traditional communities requires this passion and energy. But I found myself wondering how *Jesus* would hear Paul's passionate polemic. Would he cringe at times, as I did, knowing how such polemics can lead to self-righteous injuries of us all in frail (fallen) human communities? Would he sigh in sadness that the separations, which had to be made for the sake of a multinational extension of covenant relationship for all, would yet exact such suffering and violent dehumanization for centuries to come? These questions came alongside familiar pieces I now hear with different ears. I still hear Paul proclaiming Christ crucified and risen as a unique manifestation of God's promise and fulfillment of prophecies. I hear him differentiating a promise for this new community in terms both Mosaic and (eventually) Christian. But the law is not remotely opposed to the promises of God. As Paul himself says, "Certainly not!" Where Paul's situation and fidelity to his experience of Christ push him to polarize law and faith, my situation and fidelity to experience of Christ require a *closer* relationship between law and faith. There *is* life in the law. I know that to be true.

I am not disputing Paul or the centuries of Pauline tradition that come through the hallowed halls of my patristic (and maternal) forbears. I do see anew, however, the difficulties in abiding by polemical scripture that prevents us from learning more deeply embodied truths at table with one another. The stark contrasts necessary and faithful to God's purposes in first century C.E. no longer fit the realities of faith and practice to which I have been led, which have given my life and work a vibrant significance and irresistible compassion. A surrender to the law can result in life *for a Christian outsider companioned by the observantly Jewish.*

Conclusion

It will take a while before I understand all the fruits of these endeavors, but for now, I am newly aware of a beautiful wisdom within some expressions of *kashrut* observance and the ways this wisdom can be misused as an intra- or inter-traditional weapon of disconnection or separation. Though I remain a Christian outsider, I know in my own experience that *kashrut* is an intensely intimate wisdom and site of struggle of a group of people with a tradition, a heritage, and a vocation (accepted or resisted) to be a blessing to others. These are not "my people," nor do I know *kashrut* as some Jews do. Still, I yearn to testify within my own tradition's habits: to an ancient wisdom that honors life and its sacrifice for others' nurture, to the companionships that allowed me to encounter this wisdom, and to the beautiful complexity of living within such wisdom surrounded by "others" and "outsiders," many of whom have been hostile over the centuries.

A much clearer image emerges too for what habits of mind are likely to emerge between scripturally authoritative Christians and *kashrut*-observant Jews at table together. I inherited habits focused upon law and restrictions, artificially polarized against freedom. For all those that informed this study, *kashrut* is not primarily an observance of law but both gift and wrestling, an ever-present negotiation of identities internal and external, within Jewish life as that life is lived in civic spaces. Outsider understandings rooted in "the law" are not remotely sufficient for understanding it. Sitting at table together—for those who are even willing to enter into such fellowship—requires much deeper awareness on both sides about such inherited habits of mind. Speaking only from the view I have, as a Christian outsider, I see this lack of awareness without blame or judgment. Scriptural polemics have created, intentionally or not, habits of derision and of presumption oblivious to the lived reality that *kashrut* has a powerful wisdom to it, even if (perhaps especially because) "we" cannot conceive it within our own traditional categories.

In sum, I would not be who I am today without this Jewish wisdom, although I know it will never be "mine." Jewish companions invited me to their tables, holding me in their distinctive wisdom in a way I yet recognized in faith because the table is central in my tradition. Did I become Jewish while sitting at table in a Jewish manner? Of course not. Am I a better Christian, with a deeper understanding of Jesus' radical hospitality at table, shaped by rabbinic wisdom not his own? You decide. For my part, the expressive theological delight that has arrived, strengthening devotion in my own tradition in communion with those "outside" of it, is Spirit-fruit enough for me.

Notes

1. See especially Lise Stern, *How to Keep Kosher: A Comprehensive Guide to Understanding Jewish Dietary Laws*, William Morrow (HarperCollins), 2004, but several other texts offer historical, halakhic, and practical perspectives, that is, David C. Kraemer, *Jewish Eating and Identity Through the Ages* (London: Routledge, 2007), and David M. Freidenreich, *Foreigners and Their Food: Constructing Otherness in Jewish, Christian, and Islamic Law* (Berkeley: University of California Press, 2011).

2. "Orthodox" remains slippery in any summary sense, precise only in context. I intend a definition broader than many Orthodox Jews prefer, narrower than Reform, Conservative, Reconstructionist (or other) Jews' observance of *kashrut*. Participants were invited based upon identifiably Orthodox observance but not excluded if outside of institutional-rabbinate Orthodox Judaism. A Christian use of "orthodox," uncapitalized, refers to conciliar Christian perspective with commitment to historic faith community before and after (post-) modernity, amidst all the conceptual–spiritual complexity that entails.

3. Two are rabbis, three serve in institutions of education (two in K-12 schools, one in higher education), three engage in the study or practice of law, four in finance or business, three serve in helping professions (non-profit and/or psychological), two practice medicine as physicians, and two are writers. Seven are wives and mothers, nine are husbands and fathers, and all but three participants have children. Strands of cultural heritage were woven throughout the interviews, from "Old World" piety and laments, to Jewish American identity tensions, to eco-*kashrut* and general "foodie" cultures common between participants and the researcher.

4. "Table fellowship" is a loaded term in Christian theological circles, of course, bringing sacramental and liturgical nuances that undergird my interest if not this inquiry, per se. Here I simply mean sharing food and beverage in a multitude of circumstances, governed by specifications of (Modern) Orthodox *kashrut*.

5. An Orthodox custom I am more than delighted to "borrow" for the purposes of this and any future writing along an invited companionable way.

6. Susan Fishkoff, *Kosher Nation: Why More and More of America's Food Answers to a Higher Authority* (New York: Schocken, 2010).

7. See http://www.instituteforhabitsofmind.com/ (accessed Jan 27 2012).

8. Mary Boys and Sara Lee, *Christian and Jews in Dialogue: Learning in the Presence of the Other* (Woodstock, VT: Skylight Paths, 2006).

9. A Reconstructionist colleague spurred this learning, teaching me that Jews who do not observe *kashrut* in Orthodox manner are no less Jewish, which is admittedly an intense debate within global Jewry. I have little interest in definitions of Jewishness, however. My inquiry focused upon *kashrut* itself, lodged in textual traditions and communal practice.

CROSSCURRENTS

WHO SPEAKS FOR EUROPE'S MUSLIMS?
The Radical Right Obstacle to Dialogue

Todd H. Green

When news broke of a killing spree in Norway in July 2011, Muslims across Europe held their breath. Some prominent media outlets initially speculated that the perpetrator(s) likely had ties to Islamic extremism.[1] Once again, Muslims appeared to be in the position of having to defend themselves and their faith over against the actions of a minority.

These early reports turned out to be wrong. Neither Al Qaeda nor Islamic terrorists carried out the attacks. The culprit was Anders Breivik, one of Norway's "own," and he identified not as a Muslim but as a Christian. However, "Christian terrorism" does not sit well in the minds of many Westerners, so a debate ensued over whether Breivik was who he said he was. Church leaders, conservative bloggers, and prominent media personalities chimed in to protest any suggestion that Breivik could be considered a Christian. They noted how Breivik rejected most orthodox Christian beliefs in favor of a diluted "cultural Christianity." They pointed out that he was not so much interested in a personal relationship with God as he was in tying his own battles against immigration and multiculturalism to Europe's medieval crusading heritage and the violent restoration of a monocultural Europe. Breivik, it was concluded, was not a true believer. As *Fox News*'s Bill O'Reilly opined, "No one believing in Jesus Christ commits mass murder."[2]

These exhaustive efforts to discredit Breivik's Christian identity fell on sympathetic ears, but were they really necessary? Were Christians in any real danger of being convicted by the Western media or the court of public opinion for Breivik's crimes? The answer is no. The guilt-by-association principle does not apply to Christians.

This same courtesy is rarely extended to Europe's Muslims. Many Europeans (and Americans) readily associate Islam with violence, and the roots of this identification run deep in European history. A master narrative of Muslims as the threatening "Other," the antithesis of all that Europe holds dear, has been in the works for over a millennium and has found a solid place in modern European history. Edward Said famously made this point in *Orientalism* (1978), and a new generation of scholars has developed, expanded, and nuanced his insights.[3] But this scholarly attention to an anti-Islam narrative has not eliminated its acceptance or plausibility. If anything, the rise of radical right political parties in recent decades has strengthened and reinforced the narrative and given credence to the widespread belief that Samuel Huntington was right, that a "clash of civilizations" between Islam and the West is inevitable in the post-Cold War era.[4]

A major casualty of the radical right's emergence as a viable political force in Europe is dialogue. The radical right exploitation of the anti-Islam narrative for political gain contributes to and exacerbates a climate of fear and hostility toward Muslim minority communities, and it weakens the commitment of many European governments and citizens to multiculturalism. In such a climate, many non-Muslims will fail to perceive Muslims as potential or necessary dialogue partners who enrich the European cultural landscape. Instead, Muslims will be viewed as threats to European values and identity. And you do not dialogue with a threat; you control or contain it, and if it comes to it, you eliminate it.

The rise of the radical right
The rise of the radical right is inexplicable apart from the increase in Muslim immigrants and residents in postwar Europe. Muslims initially came as manual laborers. In the case of the United Kingdom and France, the source of this labor was from former colonies (i.e., the Indian subcontinent and the Maghreb, respectively). Before long, other countries were recruiting guest workers from regions with significant Muslim populations. By the late 1960s, many of Europe's Muslims were here on what most considered a temporary basis. This began to change by the 1970s. Family reunification, along with larger numbers of asylum seekers and refugees, led to a more

permanent Muslim population. These changing demographics, coupled with birth rates higher than the "native" population, contributed to Islam's significant growth. By the turn of the twenty-first century, Islam ranked as the second largest religion in many parts of Western Europe, with estimates of Muslims ranging from thirteen to twenty-five million in European Union (EU) nations, constituting 3–5 percent of the population.[5] In some individual nations, such as France, Germany, and the Netherlands, 5–6 percent of the population consists of Muslims.[6]

With a more permanent Muslim population came a more visible presence for Islam. Muslims began asserting their religious identities into the public sphere through distinctive dress, the building of mosques, observing daily prayer, practicing halal, etc. This increasing visibility became one of the factors leading to the changing fortunes of radical right political parties across Europe. Of course, other factors contributed to the conditions for the radical right's growth, including postindustrial economies, globalization, rising unemployment, and a decline in national identity in the wake of European integration. But the rise of the radical right is inexplicable apart from Islam's growing visibility.[7] Antonis Ellinas notes that the radical right quadrupled its support in twenty years. From averaging 2 percent of the vote in 1985, radical right parties had acquired 8.5 percent of the vote by 2006.[8] They now constitute the second or third largest political parties in countries such as Norway, Denmark, the Netherlands, and Austria. In Switzerland, a radical right party, the Swiss People's Party, has the largest representation in parliament.

Anti-immigrant and anti-Muslim sentiment is extremely common in radical right rhetoric, though I must make it clear that the radical right certainly did not create *ex nihilo* anxiety over the presence of Muslims or Islam in Europe. But the radical right has tapped into this fear in a powerful way and mobilized portions of the electorate based on it.

Radical right parties have been aided in their efforts on three fronts. First, they have benefited from the celebrity and attention given to Europe's two most famous former Muslims: Salman Rushdie and Ayaan Hirsi Ali. It is telling that those who are able to speak about Islam, and to be heard when they speak, are Muslims who are no longer Muslims. Hirsi Ali in particular reinforces the narrative of the incompatibility between Islam and the West, and her status as a former "insider" strengthens her credentials and gives added legitimacy to her views.

Second, the rise of the radical right has led some of Europe's most prominent politicians to move to the right on issues of immigration and Islam. Chancellor Angela Merkel of Germany insists that her country's multicultural approach has "utterly failed,"[9] while British Prime Minister David Cameron blames multiculturalism for "the weakening of our collective identity."[10] It is politically fashionable across Europe to criticize if not reject outright the merits of multiculturalism, and in a European context, criticism of multiculturalism is pretty much synonymous with criticism of Muslims.

The third way in which radical right parties have been helped in their political war against Muslims involves media coverage. Radical right rhetoric routinely finds a home in major newspapers, television news programs, and social media. I agree with those scholars who insist that intense media attention contributes at least to the initial rise of populist parties and likely plays a role in sustaining some degree of public interest in them.[11] The same holds true for individual radical right personalities. As Ian Buruma argues in a *New York Times* editorial, the media coverage of Geert Wilders, leader of the Party for Freedom in the Netherlands, and his anti-Islam hate speech made him into a major right-wing voice in his country and indeed across Europe. "If not for his hatred of Islam," Buruma writes, "Geert Wilders would have remained a provincial Dutch parliamentarian of little note."[12]

Why does this matter? It matters because the media participates in the construction of what the public perceives as real. In the case of Muslim minorities, "coverage in the media is often the only source for the formation of audience opinions, because many media recipients hardly have any direct contact or experience with Muslims."[13] In the words of the sociologist Michael Schudson:

> Journalists normally work with materials that real people and real events provide. But by selecting, highlighting, framing, shading, and shaping in reportage, they create an impression that real people—readers and viewers—then take to be real and to which they respond in their lives.[14]

To the extent that the media highlights the voices of right-wing politicians and frames their anti-Muslim discourse within the larger narrative of an inevitable conflict and incommensurability between Islam and the

West, the end result is a constructed reality that is simultaneously divorced from reality—at least from reality as articulated and experienced by many of Europe's Muslims.

The master narrative of Islam

If Muslims cannot speak for themselves (or at least be heard when they speak), and if the radical right dominates the narrative of Islam in Europe, the question now becomes: What is this narrative? In other words, how does the radical right tell the story of Islam? Radical right pronouncements frequently invoke four overlapping descriptors in their portrayals of Islam: violent, intolerant, anti-democratic, and misogynist. Let us take a brief look at how these motifs make their way into radical right discourse.

A typical statement on Islam's inherently violent nature can be found in a speech given by Geert Wilders in Berlin last year. Reacting to the Norway attacks carried out by Breivik, Wilders condemned the man behind the killings, but in the process he took the opportunity to sharpen the contrast between Islam and the West on violence:

> The Oslo murderer falsely claims to be one of us. But he is not one of us. We abhor violence. We are democrats. We believe in peaceful solutions.
>
> The reason why we must reject Islam is exactly Islam's violent nature. We believe in democracy. We fight with the force of our conviction, but we never use violence.[15]

Wilders's public statements on this score have not gone unchallenged. In 2009, he was charged with (and later acquitted of) hate speech for some of these statements and for his film *Fitna*, in which he intersperses citations from the Quran with media clips and newspaper headlines portraying Muslims engaged in acts of violence, including the 9/11 attacks. The media coverage of the trial certainly helped to publicize and reinforce the film's central message that the very "nature" of Islam, indeed the source of its doctrine, has led to the terrorism that we see in the world today.

But *Fitna*'s success in perpetuating the narrative of violence is unthinkable apart from a series of violent events from the past few decades that have saturated the Western media and have been tied by many journalists as well as political and cultural elites to one common source:

Islam. The Iranian Revolutions, the Persian Gulf War, 9/11 and the war on terror, Theo van Gogh's murder in Amsterdam, the Madrid and London train bombings, the Danish cartoon publications—public discourse concerning these events inevitably revolves around the "problem" of violence in Islam. To take just one example, the Danish "cartoons that shook the world" in 2005 and 2006 did so not only because they were visual depictions of the Prophet Mohammed but also because of *how* he was depicted.[16] In the most egregious example, a drawing of the Prophet with a bomb in his turban was published and republished in numerous Western media outlets. Islam's central figure was presented to the world as a terrorist.

The context for publishing the Danish cartoons in 2005 is worth mentioning because it points to the second motif: intolerance. The editor-in-chief of *Jyllands-Posten*, Carsten Juste, solicited drawings of the Prophet to test self-censorship in the Danish media and to illustrate a larger point: Denmark and the West valued tolerance and difference of opinion; Muslims are incapable of such tolerance. The twelve drawings of "The Face of Muhammad" were intended to reinforce this point.[17]

Another example of how this motif functions in radical right politics comes from Switzerland. Two leaders from the Swiss People's Party's, Ulrich Schlüer and Oskar Freysinger, made the intolerance of Islam a central point in the anti-minaret campaign that led to a ban on constructing minarets in 2009. When a television reporter equated minarets with church steeples and suggested that banning the former would thus constitute religious discrimination, Schüler responded that the two religions represent two different sets of values: "I think Christianity is an attitude of freedom, of recognizing different meanings, of tolerance. Islam has nothing to do with tolerance."[18] Freysinger echoed these sentiments by insisting that minarets are "visible symbols of an unconditional religious claim and the intolerance connected with that."[19] Such messages drive home the larger point often intended by the radical right—Europe is rooted in tolerance, but Europe can no longer afford to tolerate the intolerant (read Muslims).

Freysinger, like many radical right politicians, connected his views on Islam's violence and intolerance with the third motif: Islam's opposition to democracy and its aggressively political (as opposed to religious) nature. He argued that minarets are not innocent religious structures but in fact function as "the flags that generals place on strategic military maps to identify a conquered territory."[20] Islam is a political ideology bent on conquest and domination, and in the end, *sharia* law, not democracy, will govern Europe if steps are not taken to fight off the Muslim enemy.

Filip Dewinter, a leader in the Flemish Interest Party, typifies how right-wing politicians invoke *sharia* law to stir up fear of Islam's totalitarian nature. He argues that once *sharia* law is observed in a few instances, it will spread and eventually smother democracy:

> This introduction of *sharia*, of Islamic law, is only the first phase. Second, Muslims will demand that *sharia* become a part of our civil code. And at the end, there is only *sharia*. The holy war—the *jihad* —against the Western enemy is a duty for every Muslim.[21]

The assumed inability of Islam to embrace democracy has drastic consequences according to many radical right politicians, especially for women (our fourth motif). As the late Jörg Haider of the Austrian Freedom Party put it, "Human rights and democracy are as incompatible with the Muslim religious doctrine as is the equality of women."[22] Misogyny is built into Islam, and because Islam does not give a voice to "the people," especially women, it will forever oppress members of "the second sex." The bans on *hijabs* and *burqas* in some parts of Europe reflect just how widely accepted this narrative is. The assumption behind these bans is that no Muslim woman would ever choose to wear a *hijab* or *burqa*.

Dewinter has turned this assumption into a public campaign in Belgium called "Women Against Islamization." He notes that "[w]omen are always the first victims of Islam. We want to make clear that they have a choice." To illustrate this choice, he recently arranged for his teenage daughter to be photographed in a *burqa* that covered her head and backside, while the rest of her body was exposed and bikini-clad. The poster version of this picture has three Dutch words written across her bikini top that, translated into English, read: "Freedom or Islam?" The words plastered across her bikini bottom: "You choose!"[23]

Perhaps, the most powerful voice chastising Islam for its misogyny and its oppression of women is Ayaan Hirsi Ali. Originally from Somalia, Hirsi Ali sought and was granted political asylum in the Netherlands in the early 1990s. She eventually entered into politics, first as a member of the center-left Labor Party, then switching to the more socially conservative

People's Party for Freedom and Democracy. She served in the Dutch Parliament from 2003 to 2006, but was forced to resign after a controversy arose over whether she falsified statements on her initial asylum application.

In many ways, Hirsi Ali is a star of sorts among the radical right, at least when it comes to her statements on Islam. Her status as a former Muslim "insider" gives her added authority on all matters pertaining to Islam. And what does she have to say about her former religion, particularly in regard to its views on women? Predictably, she argues that Islam and the West are diametrically opposed in their views of women.

> As a woman in the West I have access to education. I have a job...I can marry the man of my choice, or I can choose not to marry at all...I can have an abortion. I can own property....I can have an opinion on the moral choices of others and express my opinion... This is what makes the West so great.
>
> In Muslim lands...women are denied education, have no job, and are forced into marriage with strangers. In the name of Islam, women are denied the right to their bodies...They have no rights to abortion...They cannot own property, trade, or travel without the risk of robbery or rape...This obsession with subjugating women is one of the things that makes Islam so reprehensible."[24]

Hirsi Ali's condemnation of Islam for its treatment of women achieved international notoriety in the short film *Submission*. Hirsi Ali wrote the film's script and collaborated with the filmmaker Theo Van Gogh on the film's production. *Submission* dramatized the subjugation of Muslim women in Islam through four monologues. Each monologue is voiced by an actress who has been a victim of misogyny and abuse at the hands of Muslim men and, by implication, Allah. Evidence of this abuse is inscribed on her body in the form of bruises and lashes. Justification for this violence is also "inscribed" on her body in the form of Quaranic verses.

The film aired on Dutch television in August 2004. Just over two months later, Mohammed Bouyeri, a Dutch-Moroccan Muslim, killed Van Gogh and attached to his body a note condemning the film and threatening Hirsi Ali. In the aftermath of the Van Gogh murder, the film has attracted international attention and criticism. Even so, the media attention given to the film and to its violent aftermath reinforces the "clash of civilizations" narrative that radical right politicians are so eager to exploit, a narrative that posits a violent, intolerant, anti-democratic, and misogynist religion over against a West rooted in freedom, democracy, and equality of the sexes.

I have briefly outlined four of the most reoccurring motifs in the radical right's narrative of Islam. Perhaps, a fifth could be added—Islam as monolithic and incapable of reform. Indeed, this assumption is voiced fairly often in the radical right's anti-Islam discourse and, like the other motifs, has some resonance in the broader public. I have addressed this misperception elsewhere, and for the sake of space, I will not analyze it in detail here.[25] What I can state about this motif is that it functions in many ways to tie together the other four. If Islam is incapable of reform, its views on violence, democracy, women, etc., will never change. Practically speaking, this implies that there is no hope that Muslims can ever become dialogue partners or contribute anything of worth to contemporary Europe. They are *stuck* in a barbaric, medieval religion that imprisons them in barbaric, medieval values.

The radical right narrative and its impact on dialogue

Before addressing the impact of this narrative, let me make several points in light of the preceding discussion. First, while my focus has been on radical right politicians, I recognize that theirs is not the only voice in the anti-Islam narrative. The motifs I have discussed surface in more moderate political and religious quarters. I have already alluded to the likes of Cameron and Merkel, and others could be added to this list, including the former French president Nicolas Sarkozy and the former Italian Prime Minister Silvio Burlusconi. Even Pope Benedict XVI insinuated in his Regensburg address from 2006 that Islam is rooted in violence and has been spread through coercive force.[26] The radical right does not have a monopoly on the anti-Islam narrative, nor does it bear sole responsibility for its perpetuation and negative impact.

Second, I am fully aware that the radical right's anti-Islam narrative is not the only show in town. There are plenty of endeavors by politicians, religious leaders, and ordinary citizens throughout Europe to contribute other voices and to offer alternative narratives that are more reflective of Muslim experiences and convictions. These efforts should be applauded, and I do believe they are bearing fruit. Yet in many of these instances, the voices in question that gain a public hearing are often not Muslim. Those who speak out publicly in defense of Muslims are frequently allies and not "insiders." This raises once again the challenge of dialogue. How can dialogue with Europe's Muslims really progress if the voices of Muslims are not heard (or heard less frequently) than others who speak favorably on their behalf?

Third, even when the radical right narrative is being challenged in public discourse, it still predominates. Those who challenge the narrative must do so within a framework that has already established Islam and Muslims as the problematic "Other." For this reason, challenges to the narrative often risk falling into the habit of lifting up the "good Muslim" to offset the image of the "bad Muslim." While the motivation for this is understandable, the end result is often the reinforcement of the master narrative. As Jocelyne Cesari describes it, "[t]he fact that Muslims must be named as good or law abiding means that there is an underlying assumption that Muslims are potential troublemakers."[27]

Finally, let me point out once again that the radical right did not invent the anti-Islam narrative. But I agree with David Art that the radical right has "a startling ability to set the agenda on issues such as asylum, immigration quotas, integration requirements, and citizenship laws."[28] The radical right voice is being heard and absorbed across the political spectrum.

Clearly, the radical right narrative has detrimental effects on the willingness of non-Muslims to dialogue with Muslims. The narrative feeds and reinforces a construction of Islam as the threatening "Other." It also contributes to a political climate that resists finding any merit in multiculturalism and that ultimately gives rise to discrimination, racial profiling, and restrictions on religious liberty for Muslims. In this climate, engaging Muslim voices or experiences are not real options for non-Muslims. Muslims become a problem to be solved, not possible or promising conversation partners.

For their part, some Muslims and Muslim leaders are persevering despite this climate of suspicion and hostility and endeavoring to build bridges with host countries and establish a framework for fruitful dialogue. But clearly, what I have been describing has made plenty of Muslims understandably resentful toward the non-Muslim majority.

The intolerant climate that is perpetuated by radical right narratives and, in some cases, confirmed by public opinion and actions has sent Muslims the message that their voices and their religion are not welcome. It is little wonder why many Muslims, including second- and third-generation children of Muslim immigrants, are increasingly unwilling to dialogue with the majority population.

Solutions to this dilemma are not easy. The interfaith networks that have sprouted across Europe are helping, as are the voices of courageous politicians who are willing to stand up and resist, as opposed to co-opt, the radical right's rhetoric on multiculturalism, immigration, and Islam. I am also encouraged by the increasing attention that Islamophobia as an epidemic is receiving not only by scholars but by community initiatives, anti-racism and anti-defamation organizations, government commissions, Amnesty International, and even the United Nations.[29] My own conviction, or at least my hope, is that in time, this increasing attention to Islamophobia will generate much better questions among the public, such as: Who speaks for Europe's Muslims? What do they say? Who/what is included in the narrative? Who/what is excluded? For what purposes? Once critical reflection upon these questions penetrates into the media coverage and public discourse concerning Islam, only then can the radical right's anti-Islam narrative be problematized and resisted and the voices of Europe's diverse communities of Muslims finally heard.

Notes

1. *The New York Times*, *The Washington Post*, and the *BBC*, among others, initially published stories online suggesting that Muslim terrorists were involved in the killings. See Glenn Greenwald, "The Omnipresence of Al Qaeda and Meaninglessness of 'Terrorism,'" *Salon*, July 23, 2011, available online at http://www.salon.com/2011/07/23/nyt_17/.
2. "O'Reilly Blasts Media for Branding Norwegian Terror Suspect a 'Christian Extremist,'" July 25, 2011, available online at http://www.foxnews.com/on-air/oreilly/2011/07/26/oreilly-blasts-media-branding-norwegian-terror-suspect-christian-extremist.
3. Said, Edward W. *Orientalism* (New York: Vintage Books, 1978). For an outstanding treatment of the historical roots of the anti-Islam discourse in the West, see Lyons, Jonathan. *Islam Through Western Eyes: From the Crusades to the War on Terrorism* (New York: Columbia University Press, 2012). See also Daniel, Norman. *Islam and the West: The Making of an Image* (Oxford: Oneworld, 1993); Southern, R.W. *Western Views of Islam in the Middle Ages* (Cambridge, MA: Harvard University Press, 1962); Tolan, John V. *Saracens: Islam in the Medieval European Imagination* (New York: Columbia University Press, 2002).
4. Huntington, Samuel P. *The Clash of Civilizations and the Remaking of World Order* (New York: Simon & Schuster, 1996).

5. Nachmani, Amikam. *Europe and Its Muslim Minorities: Aspects of Conflict, Attempts at Accord* (Portland: Sussex Academic Press, 2010), 15.

6. Miller, Tracy. ed., *Mapping the Global Muslim Population: A Report on Size and Distribution of the World's Muslim Population* (Pew Research Center, 2009), 31–32. A PDF version of the report is available online at http://www.pewforum.org/Mapping-the-Global-Muslim-Population.aspx.

7. This is not to suggest that immigration or the increasing visibility of Islam explains *why* radical right parties have fared better in some European countries than in others. Much of the recent scholarly literature on radical right politics has wrestled with the issue of cross-national variation in the radical right's electoral performance. Efforts to explain the discrepancies in right-wing political fortunes have typically stressed either "demand-side" or "supply-side" variables. The former argues for increasing demand for radical right policies in light of significant societal changes, including the influx of immigrants and asylum seekers, in the postwar era. The latter explains the variation by emphasizing either the differences in electoral institutions and/or the ways in which radical right parties function as agents in their own success or failure. For a representative "demand-side" work, see Betz, Hans-Georg. *Radical Rightwing Populism in Western Europe* (New York: St. Martin's Press, 1994). Two variations on the "supply-side" argument are Norris, Pippa. *Radical Right: Voters and Parties in the Electoral Market* (New York: Cambridge University Press, 2005); Art, David. *Inside the Radical Right: The Development of Anti-Immigration Parties in Western Europe* (New York: Cambridge University Press, 2011).

8. Ellinas, Antonis A. *The Media and the Far Right in Western Europe: Playing the Nationalist Card* (New York: Cambridge University Press, 2010), 4–5.

9. Quoted in Weaver, Matthew. "Angela Merkel: German Multiculturalism Has 'Utterly Failed,'" *Guardian* (UK), October 17, 2010, available online at http://www.guardian.co.uk/world/2010/oct/17/angela-merkel-german-multiculturalism-failed.

10. For a full transcript of the speech from which this excerpt is taken, see Cameron, David. "PM's Speech at Munich Security Conference," February 5, 2011, available online at http://www.number10.gov.uk/news/pms-speech-at-munich-security-conference/.

11. Mazzoleni, Gianpietro, Julianne Stewart, and Bruce Horsfield, eds., *The Media and Neo-Populism: A Contemporary Comparative Analysis* (Westport, CT: Praeger, 2003), 217–37.

12. Buruma, Ian. "Totally Tolerant, Up to a Point," *New York Times*, January 29, 2009, available online at http://www.nytimes.com/2009/01/30/opinion/30buruma.html.

13. Shooman, Yasemin and Riem Spielhaus, "The Concept of the Muslim Enemy in Public Discourse," in *Muslims in the West after 9/11: Religion, Politics and Law*, ed. Jocelyne Cesari (New York: Routledge, 2010), 202.

14. Schudson, Michael. *The Sociology of News* (New York: Norton, 2003), 2.

15. The Geert Wilders speech was given in Berlin on September 3, 2011. The English text is available online at http://geertwilders.nl/index.php/component/content/article/87-news/1764-speech-geert-wilders-in-berlin-3-September-2011-english-version.

16. See Klausen, Jytte. *The Cartoons That Shook the World* (New Haven, CT: Yale University Press, 2009).

17. Ibid.

18. Schlüer, Ulrich interviewed by Julie Hunt, "Anti-minaret Campaigner Puts Case," October 6, 2009, *swissinfo.ch*, available online at http://www.swissinfo.ch/eng/multimedia/video/Anti-minaret_campaigner_puts_case.html?cid=1012760.

19. Freysinger, Oskar. "Des Jihads Leuchttürme," May 3, 2007, available online at http://www.minarette.ch/referate/archiv-2007/des-jihads-leuchttuerme.html.
20. Ibid.
21. Quoted in "De sharia is al in Antwerpen," September 24, 2009, available online at http://www.filipdewinter.be/filip-dewinter-in-gva-de-sharia-is-al-in-antwerpen.
22. Quoted in Betz, Hans-Georg. "The Growing Threat of the Radical Right," in *Right-wing Extremism in the Twenty-First Century*, eds. Peter H. Merkl and Leonard Weinberg (Portland: Frank Cass Publishers), 84.
23. Dewsbury, Rick. "Belgian Politician Risks Muslim Backlash After Using Teenage Daughter Dressed in Burqa and Bikini for Campaign Against Islam," *Daily Mail* (UK), February 3, 2012, available online at http://www.dailymail.co.uk/news/article-2095862/Belgian-Vlaams-Belang-risks-Muslim-backlash-picture-daughter-burka-bikini.html.
24. Ali, Ayaan Hirsi. *The Caged Virgin: An Emancipation Proclamation for Women and Islam* (New York: Free Press, 2008), 162–63.
25. Green, Todd. "Does Islam Really Need a Martin Luther?," in *The Huffington Post*, July 5, 2011, available online at http://www.huffingtonpost.com/todd-green-phd/islam-martin-luther_b_884264.html.
26. Pope Benedict XVI, "Faith, Reason and the University Memories and Reflections," speech delivered at the University of Regensburg on September 12, 2006, available online at http://www.vatican.va/holy_father/benedict_xvi/speeches/2006/September/documents/hf_ben-xvi_spe_20060912_university-regensburg_en.html.
27. Cesari, Jocelyne. "Islamophobia in the West: A Comparison between Europe and the United States," *Islamophobia*, 33.
28. Art, *Inside the Radical Right*, 9.
29. I acknowledge that the term *Islamophobia* is contested in scholarly circles. It is difficult to extract fear of Islam in Europe with other prejudices such as racism or xenophobia. For an overview of the concept and how it may or may not apply to Europe and the U.S., see Cesari, "Islamophobia in the West," 21–43.

CROSSCURRENTS
I THE JEW, I THE BUDDHIST
Multi-Religious Belonging As Inner Dialogue

Mira Niculescu

In the early 1990s, a delegation of Rabbis from many denominations (from Orthodox to Reform) flew to Dharamsala to meet with the Dalai Lama. They exchanged spiritual insights, discussed similarities and differences between Judaism and Buddhism, and shared "survival tips." This interreligious dialogue was initiated by Marc Lieberman, a Buddhist Jew, who had founded an NGO for Tibetan people. Religion scholar and poet Rodger Kamenetz recounted the story of this meeting in his best seller, *The Jew in the Lotus*, to begin his exploration of the phenomenon of Jewish-Buddhists, whom he called "Jubus." Since then, the term Jubu has become a commonly used expression to designate the broad and eclectic array of Jews who practice Buddhism, and this term fails to represent the diversity of situations constituting this phenomenon. Yet academic attempts to grasp this phenomenon seem to have taken this term for granted as a new multi-religious label.

In this essay, I would like to propose an analysis that can express and address more accurately the lived realities of the so-called Jewish-Buddhists. I will show that in today's cultural context, it is more accurate to address this phenomenon in terms of an inner dialogue rather than of multi-religious belonging. Leaving aside the fascinating history and reasons for the specific connection Jews have with Buddhism, which have been addressed elsewhere (Linzer 1996, Vallely 2008, Gez 2011, Niculescu 2012), I will focus here on the performativity of this encounter: its parameters, and the way it actually "works" or rather is made to work. First, I redefine Judaism and Buddhism and explore their multi-dimensionality in today's Western contemporary societies, as both religious and secular traditions. Second, I show how, regardless of whether or not Buddhism is considered a religion, it still provokes tensions and dilemmas for Jewish-born individuals. Third, I offer a typology of inner dialogue between the reference points of Judaism and Buddhism.

Judaism and Buddhism

Two of the most frequently asked questions with respect to the Jubu phenomenon are: "What is a Jewish Buddhist?" and "Are Judaism and Buddhism compatible?" These questions require redefining Judaism and Buddhism, and examining the contemporary links between belonging, identity, and practice. Indeed in today's era of religious subjectivities, not only is it possible to practice without belonging or identifying to a tradition (for instance practicing yoga without identifying as a Hindu); it is also possible to belong and identify without practicing a religion (many contemporary Jews thus contradict Grace Davie's observation of the "Believing without belonging" [1994] phenomenon). Hence, today, practice and identification can be partial, selective, and construed in various ways.

The minimal definition of a Jewish-Buddhist designates a Jew by birth (religious or not) who practices Buddhism (whether or not he identifies with a Buddhist community). Who is a Jew and who is a Buddhist will therefore be my first question, although addressed very superficially in this essay. The first question is easier: A Jew according to *halakha* (Jewish law) is an individual born to a Jewish mother. Even Jews who live as Buddhist monastics are still considered Jews by this definition. According to Jewish tradition, the *Torah* was given to a people called Israel in a divine epiphany on Mount Sinai through Moses the prophet. Before being a religion, Judaism appears as an inherited, permanent identity.

The question of the definition of Buddhism has deep implications for the Jewish community: If it is a religion, "practicing it," that is, meditating and following Buddhist principles, can be considered a transgression of the prohibition of idolatry or *Avodah zarah*, or the "worshiping of foreign deities." This prohibition is fundamental to Judaism, as demonstrated by the second and third negative assertions of the Decalogue: A Jew is forbidden to "know other Gods" and to "make graven images" (and by extension bow to them). If Buddhism is not a religion, "practicing" should not be any more problematic than doing sports or psychotherapy. However, as we will see, as a tradition bearer with its own meaning and ritual system, Buddhism can still be viewed as contradicting Jewish precepts.

Buddhism is ontologically not a religion. First of all, "Buddhism" does not exist: It is a Western designation for the *dharma* ("path"), the philopraxis offered by Siddhartha Gautama Shakyamuni, a fifth century BCE former Hindu prince turned into a wandering ascetic on a quest to solve the existential problem of suffering. Self-directed meditation led him to see reality through the veils of the ego, and to become one with it, which was his recipe for peace. He, who was called the Buddha ("the awakened"), left a *dharma* (path) to share his discovery with others and to provide guidelines to attain this type of self-realization. So, basically, Buddhism originated as a psychophysical praxis between philosophy and therapy, performed mainly through silent-sitting meditation, to cultivate self-awareness and non-judgmental compassion. But the Buddha's heritage progressively became a religion in its Asian expressions, with deities, prayers, monks, and merit-making offerings.

"Western Buddhism" (Prebish and Baumann 2002) could not be more different; the *dharma*, already transmitted to the West by Asian teachers in secularized and universalized forms, has been even more religiously neutralized by the successive generations of Western Buddhist teachers—the majority of them Jewish. In that sense, one can say that Western Buddhism is neo-traditionalist: a new form of the original message of the Buddha.

Because Buddhism does not involve a genetic lineage in the way that Judaism does, we also need to define what makes someone a Buddhist. In his tentative identification of the different types of Western Buddhists, Thomas Tweed (2002) showed that determining who is Buddhist is nearly impossible. When a chosen praxis does not necessarily involve an inherited belonging (such as nationality), how is religious identity determined? Practice? Self-identification? Membership? In today's secular societies, these three criteria do not necessarily coalesce, as they would have in more traditional systems composed of monolithic identities. Today in the West, one can *practice* yoga (which stems from Hinduism), *identify* with Buddhism, and *belong* to a synagogue. Someone who meditates daily might not consider himself a Buddhist, while someone placing a statue of Buddha on his chimney would. Therefore, we need to ask: What are the symbolic boundaries for a Jew (bound by birth, Torah and mitzvoth), and when are they crossed? By sitting in a room with a statue of the Buddha? By reciting a Buddhist mantra? By bowing? More simply, does meditating in a Buddhist setting make one a Buddhist?

Many longtime Jewish meditators, including rabbis, have never formally entered the Buddhist community by taking the vows (taking refuge in the *Buddha*, the *dharma*, and the *Sangha* community). They simply meditate, but never with the intent to join another religion (Peltz-Weinberg 1997: 144). But for others, even taking the vows does not imply dual religious belonging, since, according to them, "Buddhism is not a religion." In sum, the boundaries are discretional. Some would bow to honor the custom of the place, understanding that it is part of Asian etiquette and not a form of idol worship, and some would not. Some would recite secular mantras, even in *Sanskrit*; others would avoid them.

Two conclusions can be inferred from this first part: First, Judaism and Buddhism can both be considered as either secular or religious. Second, when only one of the references is considered religious and the other secular, there is in principle no competition, but rather complementarity. This dichotomization of religious systems is a product of modernity's process of secularization of societies and cultures, by which religions have become "tradition tanks" (Hervieu-Leger 2000) available for individual selective appropriations.

Ultimately, the best criterion is subjective identification: the inner feeling of who one is. This is the major question posed by modernity. "Who am I?" wonders the modern individual, addressing himself with the Socratic question which has become the basis of Western philosophy. With its long processes of secularization, scientific progress and individualization, modernization has brought about the personal imperative of defining oneself in addition to being defined by one's group. This question has been rendered even more pressing in today's pluralist and globalized contexts, where the individual has become a cosmopolitan citizen: a complex being simultaneously identifying with multiple sources of identification. Indeed for Kevin Robins, in such a context, "the continuity and historicity of identity are challenged by the immediacy and intensity of global cultural confrontations. The comforts of tradition are fundamentally challenged by the imperative to forge a new self-interpretation based upon the responsibilities of cultural translation" (1991: 41 in Gillepsie

2011: 98). It is therefore the fate of contemporary individuals to fluctuate between inherited tradition and the integration of external influences. This is particularly the case for Jewish-Buddhists, in whom the two meaning and practice systems cohabit. Indeed, subjective as they may be, identities are not formed independently of their sources of identification. This, however, can become problematic for Jewish-Buddhist practitioners.

The problem
A Jewish-Buddhist will, to some extent, be linked to both Jewish and Buddhist communities. In a number of cases, the cohabitation is peaceful. This is usually the case for religious Jews for whom Buddhism is a "mindfulness" tool, or for secular Jews for whom Buddhism is their only referent meaning system, while Judaism is acknowledged as one's ethnic origin and perhaps family tradition.

Still, Judaism and Buddhism represent two very different meaning and practice systems. The former is centered on God and service to God (*avodat ha-Shem*) through *mitzvoth* (commandments), one's family, and *Am Israel* (the people Israel). The latter focuses on subjective liberation from suffering and on universal compassion. Judaism is often viewed as a textual, passionate, and family-oriented community whereas Buddhism favors silence, meditation, and a monastic ideal.

In addition to these ethical tensions, there is an extra sense in Judaism: a feeling of unavoidable belonging and responsibility, which can affect even Jews who are least affiliated: the feeling of accountability, if not for one's religion, at least for one's people (Cohen and Eisen 2000). Throughout centuries of persecution and diaspora living, the main concern for Judaism, as an ethnic religion maintained by Jewish bodies, has been the risk of extinction. In addition to these external threats, assimilation represents a more internal one: adhering to another meaning system can lead to a diminished investment in the Jewish community. For Jewish parents and institutions, this involves the risk of intermarriage, which signifies the end of a Jewish lineage if the mother is non-Jewish. This is why, since the late 1960s in the United States, in a post-Shoah, countercultural rush toward eastern spiritualities, the proportionally high number of Jews associated with Buddhism has been felt by the whole community as a new threat for Jewish continuity. While families were trying to "deprogram" their "lost" children in "cult clinics" (Linzer 1996: vxiiii), the

Lubavitcher Rebbe was publishing a *responsa*, forbidding the practice of Transcendental Meditation (1977). Soon an abundant literature on Jewish meditation appeared, which systematically condemned looking "outside," especially to the "East," for spirituality and meditation (Wolf 1997).

However, with time, two factors have helped to lessen the intensity of this problem: first, a quasi-systematic pattern of returning (*tshuva*) to Judaism as a result of the encounter with Buddhism (Linzer 1996, Vallely 2008: 20); and second, the progressive mainstreaming of Eastern spiritualities in Western cultures. Practicing yoga or meditation during the week while attending synagogue on Shabbat is no longer considered subversive. In fact, more and more mainstream Jewish denominations, including Orthodox, now offer yoga or Tai Chi classes. Nevertheless, being both Jewish and Buddhist can still cause a great deal of inner conflict for the individual who claims both identities. First, family and community disapproval is still very present in some milieus. And second, managing two systems of meaning and practice in one's everyday life and inner consciousness necessarily provokes dilemmas and cognitive dissonance.

In his research on Modern Orthodoxy in America, Samuel Heilman highlights the inner tensions experienced by individuals belonging to both modern secular culture and traditional Judaism. So much so that to overcome such a "desperate dialectic" (Heilman 1990: 141), the contemporary self, having become a *homini duplex*, has to rely on cognitive strategies aimed at the "nihilation of the dissonance," primarily through selective reinterpretation:

> Committed by inertia, circumstance, and desire to being integrated in these two fundamentally antithetical worlds, [they] (…) spent a great deal of their energies organizing their lives so as to minimize the conflicts inherent in their dualism. (Heilman 1990: 143)

This depiction could be applied, word for word, to the situation of the Jewish-Buddhists. Only the cognitive gap to be filled is, in this case, much deeper. This is mainly due to the ambiguous position of Buddhism as a "non-religious-yet-'spiritual,'" practice, which retains many ritual forms, namely bowing, mantra, and sutra chanting. In addition, the concept of spirituality is in itself equivocal: Even if they stand outside religious institutions, so-called "spiritual practices" do not necessarily belong to the secular world either. Ultimately, spiritual practices, in terms of their nature as systems of meaning and of ritual, sit alongside or compete with religions.

For Jewish-Buddhists, then, the interiorized coexistence of both meaning systems can create contradictions. For instance, should one walk to the synagogue on Saturday morning (Shabbat), or attend instead the weekly gathering of his *Sangha* to hear a *Dharma* teaching? Should one aim to live in a Buddhist monastery or to start a family? Should one pray to a creator God who has chosen the people of Israel to be a nation of priests for other nations, or should one contemplate the emptiness of concepts such as god, self and separation? The questions could go on.

In fact, as many testimonies to such dual belonging attest, the lived reality of Judaism and Buddhism can prove oppositional. For many, dual referents create significant tension, unless the traditions are combined in an intentionally complementary way. The challenge of combining or uniting religious traditions is one reason why multi-religious belonging should not necessarily be described as "identity," a term that conveys an idea of essentialist ontology, but as fluctuating internal dialogue. In this inner ongoing conversation, according to the context, the moment, and one's phase of life, one of the two references will predominate. The question of the Jewish-Buddhist phenomenon, then, cannot be understood in terms of figuring out a new identity label. It instead has more to do with how an individual brings the two practices together into a perpetually ongoing inner dialogue, in as harmonious a way as possible.

Three forms of inner dialogue: walking one's path

A dialogical notion of identity helps to capture the dynamic aspect of dual practice or belonging, in which no compromise between the two reference points of Judaism and Buddhism can be guaranteed to be permanent. It is contextual, contingent, and provisional. This is attributed to the fact that, as highlighted in many instances, today's Western religious identities are defined more as personal paths than as inherited labels (Roof 1993). This is also the case when it comes to defining one's Jewish identity (Cohen and Eisen 2000). As recent studies have shown, the contemporary religious individual is sometimes religious, sometimes less, and sees his religiosity as a trajectory rather than as a fixed identity. Therefore, the question of inner dialogue is already the cultural backdrop of this reflection on the case of Jewish-Buddhists.

Within the diversity of individual cases, three profiles of Jewish-Buddhists can be identified through the three dialogical combinations they employ. These correspond to the three levels of religious identification: identity, belief system, and practice. First, the "classic" Jewish-Buddhist pattern: the chronological stratification between an inherited Jewish cultural identity and the chosen meaning and practice system of Buddhism. The ideal-typical example of such a combination is illustrated by Marc Lieberman who describes himself as having "Jewish roots and Buddhist petals" (Kamenetz 1994: 12). This is the solution more commonly chosen by those more involved in Buddhism than in Judaism. A good example can be found in the practice of Zen *Roshi* (Master) Bernie Glassman, who organizes interfaith Zen retreats at Auschwitz. He uses his Buddhist practice to "bear witness" to the Shoah as a way to attend to his Jewish heritage.

The second pattern consists of customized hybridizations between the two meaning systems as a way to overcome conflicts and cognitive dissonance. Brenda Shoshanna's (2008) *Jewish Dharma* offers a typical example of such an endeavor: She claims to have overcome the "struggle" of her dual belonging by trying to find how each practice could enrich the other as a way to overcome their mutual contradiction. She concludes that they are "two wings of a bird" in which "engaging in Zen practice deepens Jewish experience, and helps one understand what authentic Jewish spiritual practice is," while "Jewish practice provides the humanity and warmth that can get lost in the Zen way" (2009).

Finally, the last type consists in a functional distribution between Judaism and Buddhism, where meditation is used as a tool to enhance Jewish prayer. This was first implemented by late Zen Rabbi Alan Lew. In his San Francisco synagogue, he founded a meditation group, *Makor Or* (Source of Light), where he reserved a room for silent sitting on cushions, in Zen fashion, as a preparatory practice for Jewish services. Lew explained his "return" (*tshuva*) to Judaism as a result of his Buddhist practice (Lew and Jaffe 1999). This seemingly surprising phenomenon is actually a frequent pattern for Jewish-Buddhists.

The three patterns described above have often become three successive phases of a process of, at the least, a reconciliation with one's Jewish identity and heritage, and at most, a re-embrace of Judaism as a spiritual practice. As a result, many Jewish-Buddhists actually progress through these three phases: first acknowledging one's heritage while practicing one's chosen path; then performing a cognitive hybridization of the two systems; and finally, using Buddhism's practice and mindset to enrich Jewish rituals and prayer.

Conclusion

By highlighting the social tensions and inner dilemmas provoked by the dual practice of Judaism and Buddhism, as well as by analyzing the tentative compromises made by each individual, I have tried to problematize the idealized preconceptions attached to freely crafting one's own meaning system by picking and choosing on today's religious global market. This modern discomfort is the price of today's individualistic and freer approach to religion: Unless one is being orthodox—that is to say, thoroughly following the institutionally "legitimate" discourse (doxa)—religious traditions have lost their "ontology," their sense of absolute, fixed, organic definition. They have become modeled by individual perceptions and appropriations.

Finally, one can say that in these forms of symbolic and ritual *bricolage* where subjectivity prevails, performance is more important than theology. What makes dual belonging work is dual practice, which is really a constant inner dialogue.

Works Cited

Cohen, Steven M., and Arnold M. Eisen, 2000, *The Jew Within: Self, Family, and Community in America*, Bloomington: Indiana University Press.

Davie, Grace, 1994, *Religion in Britain since 1945: Believing Without Belonging*, Oxford: Blackwell.

Gez, Yonatan, 2011, "The Phenomenon of Jewish Buddhisms in Light of the History of Jewish Suffering," *Nova Religio: The Journal of Alternative and Emergent Religions* 15(1), August, pp. 44–68.

Gillepsie, Marie, 2011, "The Role of Media in Religious Transnationalism," in Gordon Lynch, Joylon P. Mitchell, and Anna Strhan, eds., *Religion, Media and Culture: A Reader*, New York: Routledge, pp. 98–110.

Heilman, Samuel, 1990, "Constructing Orthodoxy," in Thomas Robins and Anthony Dick, eds., *In Gods We Trust; New Patterns of Religious Pluralism in America*, New Brunswick, NJ: Transaction Books, pp. 141–58.

Hervieu-Léger, Danièle, 2000, *Religion as a Chain of Memory*, Cambridge: Polity.

Kamenetz, Rodger, 1994, *The Jew in the Lotus: A Poet's Rediscovery of Jewish Identity in Buddhist India*, San Francisco: Harper.

Lew, Alan, and Sherill Jaffe, 1999, *One God Clapping: The Spiritual Path of a Zen Rabbi*, New York: Kodansha International.

Linzer, Judith, 1996, *Torah and Dharma: Jewish Seekers in Eastern Religions*, Northvale, NJ: Jason Aronson.

Niculescu, Mira, 2012, "'Find Your Inner God and Breathe' Buddhism, Popular Culture, and Contemporary Metamorphoses in American Judaism," in François Gauthier and Tuomas Matikarten, eds., *Religion in a Neoliberal Age*, London: Ashgate.

Peltz-Weinberg, Sheila, 1997, "Meditating as a Practicing Jew," in Avram Davis, ed., *Meditation From the Heart of Judaism*, Woodstock, VT: Jewish Lights, pp. 139–48.

Prebish, Charles S., and Martin Baumann, 2002, *Westward Dharma: Buddhism Beyond Asia*, Berkeley: University of California.

Roof, Wade C., 1993, *A Generation of Seekers: The Spiritual Journeys of the Baby Boom Generation*, San Francisco: Harper San Francisco.

Shoshanna, Brenda, 2000, Jewish Dharma. Interreligious Dialogue: The Website for Inter-Religious Dialogue, accessed on March 2012, http://irdialogue.org/articles/dialoguing-in-your-area-articles/on-Jewish-dharma-by-brenda-shoshanna/.

Tweed, Thomas, 2002, "Who Is a Buddhist? Night-Stand Buddhists and Other Creatures," in Martin Baumann, and Charles Prebish, eds., *Westward Dharma: Buddhism Beyond Asia*, Berkeley: University of California, pp. 17–33.

Vallely, Anne, 2008, "Jewish Redemption by Way of the Buddha," in Celia Rothenberg, and Anne Vallely, eds., *New Age Judaism*, London: Vallentine Mitchell, pp. 19–33.

Wolf, Laibl, 1997, "Meditation and the Art of Growing Your *Neshamah*," in Avram Davis, ed., *Meditation From the Heart of Judaism*, Woodstock, VT: Jewish Lights, pp. 149–56.

CROSSCURRENTS

COMPLEX RELIGIOUS IDENTITY IN THE CONTEXT OF INTERFAITH DIALOGUE

Karla Suomala

The beginning of dialogue...

In the *Life of Pi* by Yann Martel, Pi, the main character, tells the story of his extraordinary, if surreal, adventures on a lifeboat with a crew of animals. Prior to that epic journey, Pi describes his early and enduring interest in religion. By age 16, he claims Christian, Muslim, and Hindu religious identities. "The sense of community that a common faith brings to people spelled trouble for me," says Pi as he recalls an encounter between his parents, his priest, his imam, and his pandit.[1]

"'What is your son doing going to temple?' asked the priest.

'Your son was seen in church crossing himself,' said the imam.

'Your son has gone Muslim,' said the pandit."[2]

Each claiming him, the Hindu, Christian, and Muslim leaders begin to fight with each other over Pi's affiliation and then over the superiority of their respective traditions.

"That was my introduction to interfaith dialogue," says Pi.[3]

The end of dialogue...

In the "real" world, Pi's declaration of his Hindu-Christian-Muslim identity would also signal the end to his participation in interfaith dialogue. While people from different religious traditions engage with each other in a variety of ways, the term interfaith dialogue (or inter-religious dialogue) generally suggests a very specific type of engagement. As a twentieth century development primarily in the West, interfaith dialogue involves more structured and formal conversations between representatives (usually religious scholars, clergy, and institutional officials) from at least two clearly defined religious traditions with the primary objective of mutual understanding rather than conversion. Within this model, Pi—who identifies himself with more than one religious tradition—would not likely be invited to the table. This wouldn't be such an issue if Pi's religious identity remained a fictional construct, with no correspondence to real people and living communities, but that is simply not the case.

A quick glance at the population in the United States demonstrates that having a complex religious identity—an identity in which one adheres to, practices, believes in, or belongs to more than one religious tradition through inheritance and/or choice—is on the rise.[4] In the last century, for example, "the number of interfaith marriages rose in every decade, reaching highs in the 30 to 33 percent range as the twentieth century closed."[5] Diana Butler Bass points out that the children from these marriages "do not choose to belong to multiple religious communities; they simply do so by virtue of their birth."[6]

The rate of intermarriage for American Jews is even higher. Already in 2001, a striking 52 percent of Jews between the ages of 18–24 came from intermarried families.[7] And many children of intermarriage say they "simply cannot turn their backs on the non-Jewish half of their identity. Their rabbis may say they are Jewish, but in their hearts they are also whatever grandma and grandpa are," reports Leah Blankenship in *The Wisconsin Jewish Chronicle*.

Rabbi Alan Flam, former director of Brown's Hillel, thinks that this is a radically new question for the Jewish community. He notes that:

> Students are talking less about theology and more about culture. They are saying, "Wait, I have a dual identity," similar to students who may have one parent who is Asian and one who is black. They are saying, "I want to figure out a way to affirm both identities in my life."[8]

On a broader scale, the number of Americans who have adopted practices associated with Hinduism or Buddhism, such as yoga and meditation, has skyrocketed. In a recent *New York Times* article, William Broad points out that "the number of Americans doing yoga has risen from about 4 million in 2001 to what some estimate to be as many as 20 million in 2011."[9] Similarly, a 2007 National Institute of Health study indicated that over 20 million people in the United States had meditated in the previous 12 months.[10] While most of these individuals would not necessarily identify themselves as Buddhists or Hindus, they have integrated practices originating in these traditions that make their religious identities more complex or nuanced.[11]

In the face of such change, the field and practice of interfaith dialogue has taken only very tentative steps toward rethinking the future of such dialogue. For interfaith dialogue to have a meaningful role in the future, it must take Pi and those like him into account. If it does not, there won't be anyone left at the table.

Interfaith dialogue and its colonial roots

Catholic theologians Peter Phan and Catherine Cornille are among the few scholars who have even begun to take complex religious identity into consideration in their discussions of interfaith dialogue. They, however, both express doubt as to whether individuals identifying in religiously complex ways should even be included in dialogue. Phan, for example, says:

> Indeed, interreligious dialogue…may militate against multiple religious belonging since as a matter of methodology it requires that participants in interfaith dialogue preserve their distinctive religious doctrines and practices, and that they show how these are not only similar to but different from those of other faiths.[12]

Cornille takes an even stronger position, stating that "All religions are based on particular beliefs and practices that at some level or another are mutually incompatible," and as a consequence, "for most participants in dialogue, one religion in fact remains the primary object of religious identification."[13]

Phan's and Cornille's positions reflect the general consensus in the world of interfaith dialogue. As someone who has been excluded from the dialogue table, interfaith blogger Susan Miller Katz points out, "Despite our lifelong immersion in interfaith reality, interfaith children [those who inherit at least two different traditions from their parents] have rarely been formally included in the 'interfaith movement.'"[14] She goes on to suggest that interfaith children don't fit into the tried-and-true formula for interfaith discourse, a process that involves well-defined boundaries, distinct labels, and clear goals. Interfaith children, she quips, are perhaps threatening in that they seem to represent "the alarming consequence of interfaith dialogue gone wild, of tolerance turned into physical passion."[15] Their very existence challenges the nature of the categories themselves.

The categories of religious identity and affiliation used to define dialogue participants are not as innocent as they might seem, though. According to sociologist of religion Robert Orsi, the terms we use to identify religions, as well as their adherents and the meanings that we attach to them, first appeared in the "early modern era in the West amid the ruins of the religious wars between Protestants and Catholics and just when Europeans were encountering the ancient religious cultures of Asia, Africa, and the Americas."[16] The new discourses about religion and religions that emerged from this period, in which

> the dilemmas, judgments, hatreds, and longings of modern Christian history were inevitably if unconsciously embedded...became one medium for construing the peoples dominated by European nations, at home (in factories, on slave plantations, in urban working class enclaves) and abroad.[17]

In other words, the religious categories that we use today, as well as the language we use to designate those categories, largely emerged during the colonial encounter as a way to preserve the status and power of white Christians and their institutions. The term syncretism, for example, reflects the profound discomfort that white Christians had with any type of blending or mixture of European Christianity and indigenous culture. Coined by Plutarch in the first century CE, the term syncretism did not take on negative connotations until the late seventeenth century in the wake of the Reformation. When Lutheran theologian Georg Calixtus used it to propose a unification of various Protestant Churches with each other with the ultimate goal of reunion with the Catholic Church, his ideas were rejected by both Lutherans and Catholics as a "heretical and inconsistent jumble of theologies."[18] In the ensuing period of missionary expansion, syncretism came to denigrate "colonial local churches that had burst out of the sphere of mission control and begun to 'illegitimately' indigenize Christianity instead of properly reproducing the European form of Christianity they had originally been offered."[19]

Our conceptions of religious identity, both in academia and in the pew, are largely based on these older institutional models of identity and affiliation and reflect the same fears toward mixture and change as our colonial predecessors. Many religious leaders as well as theologians still talk about and study religion as if it were based upon a "unitary, organizationally defined, and relatively stable set of collective beliefs and practices" with clear definitional boundaries "that distinguish religious practices of one religious group from another's, [and view] them as mutually exclusive."[20] Within this model, religious affiliation has been understood as a sort of "master category that determines an entire set of norms for an individual member's entire faith and practice—allowing some practices as 'good' or consistent with the organization's religion and condemning others as 'bad' or even heretical."[21] This is still the case in the realm of interfaith dialogue. The result is that only those who identify as and are claimed by a single recognized religious tradition are invited to the table. Christian-Jews and Zen-Presbyterians need not apply.

New possibilities, new questions

Today, however, most sociologists would argue that religious identity, like other forms of identity, is a dynamic process through which a variety of "religious and cultural meanings are interpreted, reconstructed, and changed over time in light of new, ever-changing historical and social circumstances."[22] They employ terms such as hybrid which describes individuals formed by several interlocking religious histories and cultures, and who have learned to live with, and indeed speak from the "in-between" spaces of different religious cultures.[23] Like syncretism, the term hybrid was used pejoratively in the colonial period, but has been resurrected to emphasize the more positive aspects of mixture. In addition, scholars have more recently begun to use the term bricolage to designate individuals who choose to blend institutional and popular forms of religion or look to a variety of religious practices, beliefs, ethical systems, and traditions for inspiration. Both terms emphasize mixture and point to the fluid and multitextured nature of religious identity.[24]

that they are often employed interchangeably in literature on the subject, leading one scholar to ask: "Is our vocabulary so impoverished because there is no such thing to be described, or because we have difficulty envisaging it?"[35]

Dialogue anew

Where does all of this leave us? If we continue to conduct interfaith dialogue as if Pi and people like him didn't exist or exclude him out of a sense of religious superiority, the whole dialogue process will lose integrity. It will be founded on a convenient fiction, one that obscures our fears of change and perpetuates erroneous ideas of the nature of religious identity that privilege the few. It is too easy, argues Diana Butler Bass, "to accuse these people [with complex religious identities] of sloppy thinking or spiritual silliness, or participating in a thoughtless mélange of post-modern goofiness," when this is not necessarily (or even usually) the case.[36] Taking people with complex religious identities seriously and recognizing the contributions they can make to interfaith dialogue may be the more difficult, but definitely the more honest, and ultimately the most fruitful, course of action. Especially as those of us engaged in interfaith dialogue realize that "they" are probably "us."

Susan Katz Miller made the case in a recent *Huffington Post* piece for the inclusion of people with complex religious identities in interfaith dialogue:

> As the real world shrinks and the online world expands, we have growing opportunities to meet, to exchange ideas and to share religious perspectives. Interfaith children have intimate lifelong experience with finding and creating these connections. We see the common ground... We see the differences... We see how to create bridges of understanding. We are those bridges.[37]

Katz Miller argues further that excluding interfaith children or anyone with a complex religious identity from interfaith dialogue not only limits the contributions such individuals might make, but it can also breed religious and social conflict. According to Amartya Sen, "The increasing tendency to overlook the many identities that any human being has and to try to classify individuals according to a single allegedly pre-eminent religious identity is an intellectual confusion that can animate dangerous divisiveness."[38]

In some ways, the situation is ironic—the modern interfaith dialogue movement emerged from the ashes of the Shoah as a way to forge mutual understanding and compassion between individuals from different religious expressions. In the last half-century, this movement has made tremendous progress in achieving those goals, particularly among Jews and Christians. We are now at another turning point, however, and our circles of discourse must become more inclusive, in part because the first round was so successful.

Reflecting on his spiritual journey, Pi says,

> We are all born like Catholics, aren't we—in limbo, without religion, until some figure introduces us to God. After that meeting the matter ends for most of us. If there is a change, it is usually for the lesser rather than the greater; many people seem to lose God along life's way. That was not my case.

Thinking about his friend Mamaji, who has both a French and an Indian passport, Pi asks his mother, "Why can't I be a Hindu, a Christian, and a Muslim?" And why shouldn't Pi have a seat at the table?

Notes

1. Yann Martel, *The Life of Pi* (New York: Harcourt, 2001), 64.
2. Ibid.
3. Ibid., 68.
4. This is comparable to what is happening to racial categories. See Hope Yen, "Interracial Marriage in the U.S. Climbs to New High, Study Finds," Huffington Post, February 16, 2012, accessed June 2012, http://www.huffingtonpost.com/2012/02/16/interracial-marriage-in-us_n_1281229.html and Gregory Rodriguez, "President Obama: At odds with clear demographic trends toward multiracial pride," Los Angeles Times, April 4, 2011, accessed June 2012, http://articles.latimes.com/2011/apr/04/opinion/la-oe-rodriguez-column-obama-race-20110404.
5. Diana Butler Bass, *Christianity After Religion* (New York: Harper Collins, 2012), 61.
6. Ibid.
7. Pearl Beck, Ph.D., Ron Miller, Jacob B. Ukeles, *Young Jewish Adults in the United States Today*, American Jewish Committee (AJC), September 2006, accessed June 2012, http://www.ajc.org/atf/cf/%7B42D75369-D582-4380-8395-D25925B85EAF%7D/YoungJewishAdultsUS_102006.pdf.
8. Michael Lukas, "Divisible Jewishness," *New Voices: National Jewish Student Magazine*, April 17, 2002, accessed June 2012, http://www.newvoices.org/campus?id=0066
9. William Broad, "How Yoga Can Wreck Your Body," *New York Times*, January 5, 2012, accessed June 2012, http://www.nytimes.com/2012/01/08/magazine/how-yoga-can-wreck-your-body.html?pagewanted=all.

10. National Center for Complementary and Alternative Medicine, "Meditation: An Introduction," updated June 2010, accessed June 2012, http://nccam.nih.gov/health/meditation/overview.htm

11. This data does not imply that all meditation practices in the United States are directly derived or influenced by Buddhism; many other world religious expressions also include meditation. However, it can be said that many of the meditation practices currently in use were at least inspired by an interest in or connection to Eastern meditative traditions.

12. Peter Phan, "Multiple Religious Belonging: Opportunities and Challenges for Theology and Church," *Theological Studies* 64 (2003), 496–497.

13. Catherine Cornille, "Double Religious Belonging: Aspects and Questions," *Buddhist-Christian Studies* 23 (2003), 45–46.

14. Susan Katz Miller, "Why Include Interfaith Children in Interfaith Dialogue?" *Huffington Post*, July 8, 2012, accessed June 2012, http://www.huffingtonpost.com/susan-katz-miller/why-include-interfaith-ch_b_893526.html

15. Ibid.

16. Robert Orsi, *Between Heaven and Earth: The Religious Worlds People Make and the Scholars Who Study Them* (Princeton, NJ: Princeton University, 2006), 178.

17. Ibid.

18. Charles Stewart, "Syncretism and Its Synonyms: Reflections on Cultural Mixture," *Diacritics*, 29, no. 3 (1999): 46.

19. Ibid.

20. Meredith McGuire, *Lived Religion: Faith and Practice in Everyday Life* (Oxford: Oxford University, 2008), 186.

21. Ibid.

22. Dzintra Ilishko, "Pedagogical Challenges for Educating an Authentic Religious Identity and Responsible Pluralism," in *Religious Education in a World of Religious Diversity*, ed. by Wilna A. J. Meijer et al. (Berlin: Waxmann, 2009), 43.

23. Stuart Hall, "New Cultures for Old," in *A Place in the World? Places, Culture and Globalization*, Doreen Massey and Pat Jess, eds. (Oxford: Oxford Univ. Press: 1996), 206. See also Melissa Butcher and Mandy Thomas, "Ingenious: Emerging Hybrid Youth Cultures in Western Sydney," in *Global Youth?: Hybrid Identities, Plural Worlds*, Pam Nilan and Carles Feixa, eds. (London, New York: Routledge, 2006), 53–71.

24. Karel Dobbelaere, "Secularization," in *Encyclopedia of Religion and Society*, William H. Swatos Jr., ed. (Lanham, MD: AltaMira Press, 1998), 455. L. Voye, "From Institutional Catholicism to 'Christian Inspiration,'" in *The Post-war Generation and the Establishment of Religion*, Jackson Carroll, W.C. Roof, David Roozen, eds. (Boulder, CO: Westview, 1995), 201.

25. James R. Beebe, "Bricolage: The Postmodern Eclectic. Identifying Syncretistic Religious Cosmologies," in *The Psychologies in Religion: Working with the Religious Client*, E. Thomas Dowd and Steven Lars Nielsen, eds. (New York: Springer, 2006), 20.

26. McGuire, 4.

27. Belonging, as opposed to other forms of claiming or appropriating religious identity, "entails a host of shared commitments, shared in a wider community of persons whose appropriations and meanings derived from them come close to one's own." See Jeffery Carlson, "Double Religious Belonging: A Process Approach: Responses," *Buddhist-Christian Studies* 23 (2003), 78.

28. Robert Schreiter, "Christian Identity and Interreligious Dialogue: The Parliament of the World's Religions at Chicago, 1993," unpublished paper, cited by Jeffery Carlson, "Double Religious Belonging: A Process Approach: Responses," *Buddhist-Christian Studies* 23 (2003), 77–78.
29. Phan, 497.
30. Ibid., 498.
31. Ibid., 500, 519.
32. Cornille, 45.
33. Paul Knitter, *With Buddha I Could Not Be a Christian* (Oxford: Oneworld, 2009).
34. Carlson, 79.
35. Stewart, 42, citing Barbara Abou-El-Haj, "Languages and Models for Cultural Exchange," in *Culture, Globalization and the World System: Contemporary Conditions for the Representation of Identity*, ed. Anthony King (Binghampton: Dept. of Art and Art History, State University of New York, 1991), 143–44.
36. Butler Bass, 61.
37. Katz Miller.
38. Ibid., citation from Amartya Sen, *Identity and Violence: The Illusion of Destiny* (New York: W. W. Norton, 2006).

CROSSCURRENTS

EMBODYING TRADITION
Liturgical Performance as a Site for Interreligious Learning

Emma O'Donnell

Theological discourse has traditionally been cognitive and verbal from start to finish; as indicated by its etymology, it communicates through the word, and these words are themselves commentary on other words. For the most part, this is also the case in interreligious theological ventures such as comparative theology, which is often based on textual studies, and in interreligious dialogue, which is generally understood to be an oral or textual communication. Yet, despite the seemingly circular entrapment of theology within propositional language, systematic verbal discourse represents only a fraction of religious faith as it is experienced by practitioners. Faith is more than intellectual assent to propositions; faith is experiential.

For this reason, a theological mode or "language" that expresses a religious tradition as it is *experienced* may be capable of penetrating elements of faith that are not readily accessible through the traditional propositional mode of theology. A context for such a theological language is found in liturgy, where the full content of liturgical performance is not communicated by words alone, but is both formed and enacted ritually, through physical gesture, vocalization, repetition, and an engaged involvement of the person acting in time.

I argue in this essay that a theological mode rooted in liturgical performance—that is, a mode that "reads" the symbolic, embodied language of liturgical performance, and that seeks to grasp and communicate its complex extra-verbal content—has much to offer interreligious theological ventures. If liturgy is a fertile ground of religious formation and expression, it follows that situating comparative theology and interreligious dialogue in liturgy may open the door to new directions in interreligious learning. Yet, the full content of liturgy cannot be readily accessed by one outside of the religious tradition, as liturgical performance is by nature an activity bounded by tradition and the specificity of religious identity. In the pages that follow, I will talk about how this very quality paradoxically may lead to interreligious learning. The limits to understanding reveal to us something of the nature of liturgical experience, and of the incommensurability and dignity in difference of religious traditions.

The implications of *Lex Orandi, Lex Credendi* for interreligious learning
The mode of liturgical theology proposed here differs from the more widely used historical and textual methods of liturgical studies. Maintaining that the meaning of liturgical performance exceeds its verbal content, and that its full significance comes to be in the enactment of liturgy, this approach uses the experience of liturgical performance as its data. Rather than reading only the liturgical text, it reads the "text" of the performance or enactment, allowing the liturgy itself to speak theologically.

The notion of letting liturgical performance speak for itself rests on the idea that liturgy does not merely express previously developed theological views, but forms these views through its enactment. This is expressed by the ancient adage *lex orandi, lex credendi*, originally formulated by Prosper of Aquitaine as *ut legem credendi lex statuat supplicandi*. While the adage in its original context was intended against Semi-Pelagians and referred specifically to liturgical intercessions, in later usage, the phrase was reworded as *lex orandi, lex credendi* and took on a broader meaning, signifying the more general idea that belief is formed through liturgy.[1]

According to this concept, the voice of religious belief is spoken first in liturgical performance. In other words, liturgical performance forms belief and cultivates it through the *enactment* of believing. The adage implies that liturgy may be seen as a sort of catechism in action, and this bears an important implication for interreligious learning: if liturgy forms and speaks belief, liturgical performance may be a voice in dialogue, speaking our belief for us.

The suggestion that a ritual might speak for us, or that "we" could be considered a collective that may be spoken for as a whole, may initially seem to rob the individual of uniqueness and to replace the free individual with a codified type or a mute participant. However, the idea that liturgical performance speaks belief for us implies less a loss of uniqueness than it does a sense of interconnection, through awareness of the continuity of tradition, transmitted through community. The individual's religious identity is not autonomous, just as the individual herself is not a monad; the individual is formed by the culture, language, and tradition in which she is immersed, and her identity is thus communal, maintained through a web of interconnection.

Despite the standard claim that interreligious dialogue cannot be conducted between traditions as wholes but can only occur between individuals representing themselves as unique members of traditions, it seems that the cultural formation of belief is such that an interreligious dialogue is also, in a sense, a dialogue between traditions. Through this understanding of the formation of religious identity, interreligious dialogue becomes a conversation between communal, tradition-based identities, or at least between identities formed through the structures of cultural and religious traditions.

This theoretical framework is clearly indebted to the George Lindbeck's cultural-linguistic theory, which claims that religions function similarly to cultures and languages, shaping a person's understanding. The truths claimed by a religion are coherent within the framework of that particular religion, yet this internal coherence does not translate outside the system, leading to "incommensurable notions of truth" between traditions.[2] According to Lindbeck, this in no way negates the validity of religious truth claims, although it does set limits to the capability of fully and directly understanding the truth proclaimed by another religious system.[3]

The idea that religion functions formatively like culture, and that liturgy is formative of belief, points to promising venues for comparative theology and interreligious dialogue. Understanding liturgy to be the site of the formation of belief, as well as the process of the enactment and communication of belief, allows the voice of liturgical performance to function as a voice in interreligious learning.

The language of experience

If the full content of liturgy comes into being in its performance, the nature of the *experience* of liturgical performance must be determined. In this study, the crux of the question lies in the degree to which the real content of liturgical performance can be communicated; first, "translated" into a verbal form, and second, communicated in an interreligious context to those who do not experience it firsthand.

The term "experience" tends to be associated with individual experience and in discourse on religion is often connected to the notion of religious impulses arising from individual experience and emotion. However, while the operative meaning of the term "experience" in the context of liturgical performance certainly includes elements of individual experience, liturgical experience is also, and perhaps more importantly, communal.

For Russian Orthodox theologian Alexander Schmemann, the experience of faith refers to "the total and living experience of the Church."[4] Specifying the context in which this experience occurs, he writes that "this *experience* of the Church is primarily the experience given and received in the Church's *leitourgia*—in her *lex orandi*."[5] He concludes that experience, by this definition, is the source of theology. Schmemann's insights indicate that religious experience can indeed be seen as a communal phenomenon, received through liturgical performance, and that this communal phenomenon serves as the data of theology.

Schmemann also addresses the particular way in which the content of religious experience, situated in liturgy, is communicated theologically. Explaining that theology based on this kind of experience is not propositional, he writes "It is 'description' more than 'definition' for it is, above all, a search for words and concepts adequate to and expressive of the living experience of the Church—for *reality* and not 'propositions.'"[6] In other words, liturgical experience speaks its own language; it communicates evocatively rather than propositionally. Likewise, a theology whose source is liturgical performance must find a language with which to communicate experience rather than propositions.

The notion that liturgy speaks in a unique, non-propositional mode of communication suggests that traditional discursive theology and the language of liturgical performance not only speak in different languages, but may actually communicate different kinds of content. Whereas discursive theology tends to be concerned with meaning, expressed propositionally, liturgy communicates through its performance and thus expresses content specific to performative action.

Richard McCall makes a similar suggestion in *Do This: Liturgy as Performance*, in which he writes that liturgy asks not "what does this mean," but rather "what are we doing."[7] Behind this is the concept that ritual communicates a process of *becoming*; it expresses *doing* rather than the *being* expressed through metaphysics. If God is better understood through action or process than through the concept of metaphysical Being, as McCall suggests, then the *doing* of liturgical performance contemplates the *doing* of divine action.[8] Liturgical performance becomes a participation in the activity of which reality is constituted, and so the question of meaning is subsumed by the question asked by the performance: "what are we doing."

Interreligious dialogue in the language of liturgical performance

Having explored a theological mode based on liturgical performance, it is now time to consider the potential for situating interreligious dialogue and comparative theology within this mode. The discussion thus far has focused on the language of religious ritual, and the next step involves determining whether this language is capable of "speaking" in an interreligious or comparative context, across the borders of religious traditions.

Driving the claim that a liturgically situated theology may be a fruitful site for comparative theology and interreligious dialogue is the idea that tradition is embodied in liturgical performance. Through liturgical performance, participants "clothe" themselves in tradition, as the liturgical performance invites the participants to "put on" the tradition and enact it in such a way that they become the image of tradition. Tradition becomes enfleshed in the performance; through the gestures, words, and other performative elements, the participant's body speaks as the voice of tradition. Seen this way, liturgical performance is a dialogue waiting to happen. It is the embodied voice of a religious tradition, needing only the liturgically embodied voice of the "other" to become a dialogue leading to interreligious learning.

Practical considerations

Finally, a practical method must be found for communicating liturgical experience across religious traditions. Here, it should be made clear that this study does not advocate multi-faith liturgies, which attempt to combine the traditions of multiple religions in a single liturgy, as a site for deep interreligious learning. While these types of liturgies may have value as facilitators of social understanding, they are problematic as sites for theological learning, as the open boundaries inherent in these multi-faith liturgies lack the capacity to communicate the specificity of a religious tradition. Through their very openness, they have broken down the chain of transmission of religious particularity, through which participants perform the embodiment of religious tradition.

Rather, this study favors maintaining religiously distinct liturgical celebrations, while placing the voices of these traditional liturgical performances in dialogue. It seeks ways of communicating the content of liturgical performance across religions, while maintaining the boundaries and religious norms of traditional liturgies. Liturgy has traditionally been celebrated as an "insider" event, and upholding this pattern respects the particularity of religious traditions. This is essential if the transmission of tradition is to be maintained, for it is through this very transmission that liturgical performance allows participants to embody and communicate tradition.

The use of liturgical experience as theological data invites creative methodologies, for there is no clear or well-worn methodological path. However, a number of approaches may hold promise. Among these, consulting first-person accounts of liturgical experience may be the most direct method of accessing the data of experience. This method requires caution, however, for it risks expressing an individual, subjective experience, and may not reflect the communality of liturgical experience as it is transmitted through tradition.

The challenges that arise in gathering, interpreting, and expressing liturgical experience as theological data might be at least partially answered by interdisciplinary use of the social sciences. Anthropological understandings of social transformation, most notably as developed by Victor Turner in the concept of social drama, offer insights that point to the possibility of interpreting liturgical experience by looking at its function in social transformation. Whereas experience is interior, even in Schmemann's understanding of communal experience, social and theological transformation might be considered the external, observable element of the interior experience. Another discipline useful for the challenges of a liturgical theology rooted in liturgical performance is the field of linguistics, which provides more nuanced understandings of the symbolic language of ritual. These are just a few general indications of theological directions that might address the challenges inherent in mining insights from liturgical performance and bringing them into the field of interreligious learning.

Experiences in liturgical interreligious learning

Because liturgical performance is experiential, the language in which it speaks is elusive. It comes into being through its performance, and the content that it communicates is ultimately only completely coherent to one who engages in full confessional participation in the liturgy. I have found that this rather abstract concept becomes very evident in attempts to share my own liturgical experiences with people of other religious traditions, as well as in my attempts to experientially understand the liturgies of other traditions.

I am Catholic, and in my experiences both of inviting non-Catholics to attend mass with me and of attending the liturgies of others, I have found something surprising: *the fruit of the encounters is often the realization of the inaccessibility to the religious outsider of full liturgical experience and understanding.*

As is the case in the liturgical celebrations of many traditions, the Catholic mass is not an exposition of doctrine, but a performance that can be experienced most completely through full participation as a confessional member of the tradition. This is most clear in the Eucharist, which is taken into the body of the participants and is thus experienced in a deeply personal and internal way. In a similar manner, the entire mass is a performative act whose full content can be absorbed only in committed participation.

Despite these limits, a certain degree of participation and understanding is indeed available, and an important element in the capacity to absorb the content of a liturgical performance in another tradition often seems to reside in the degree to which the person is able to bodily participate in the actions of the liturgy. I have found this in my experiences attending Jewish liturgies, including daily prayer services, Shabbat services, and home liturgies. In each case, although immediate experience of the full significance of the liturgy was unavailable to me, I felt I was able to participate to a greater degree when I joined in the recitation or singing of texts. Through the bodily participation of engaging my voice, in rhythm with the group, I was able to at least partially overcome some of the obstacles inherent in being a religious outsider. Similarly, non-Catholic guests who have attended Catholic liturgies with me have found a deeper degree of engagement through physical participation, even by simply participating in the rhythm of standing, sitting, and kneeling. This supports the notion of liturgy as a participatory performance; that is, we must perform if we are to understand.

Conclusion

Here, we return to the paradox of liturgical performance as a site of interreligious learning: One must do it to know it, yet the nature of religious practice makes it an insider event, requiring enclosure within the sphere of religious formation for full participation. However, the beauty of this paradox lies in the fact that it contributes to interreligious learning through the limits that it reveals. The limitations revealed in interreligious liturgical experiences need not be seen simply as a door that shuts in the face of one who attempts experiential knowledge of another tradition's liturgies; rather, they can be seen as a sign pointing to the richness that lies just beyond the reach of comprehension. They point to the depth of religious experience that can be accessed only through full participation in the liturgical performance, and it may be the realization of this depth, and of its inaccessibility, that is most valuable.

This realization has valuable implications for interreligious relations: The rejection of the validity of a religious tradition is often predicated on the assumption that the truth of that tradition is easily accessible and fully understood. The mistaken claim that the full content of the religion has been adequately perceived is generally followed by judgment, in which the tradition's truth claims are deemed to be false or insufficient. Consequently, the realization of the inaccessibility of religious experience to outsiders provides a remedy to this kind of hasty judgment and rejection, and it can engender an attitude of "epistemological humility."[9] This humility becomes invaluable in interreligious dialogue and facilitates an awareness of the ultimate incomprehensibility of the religious other.

Essentially, the claim being made here is of the virtue of impossibility: The attempt to enter into the liturgical experience of the religious other leads to real interreligious learning precisely because complete entry is impossible. Interreligious learning may be most fruitful when it encounters a limitation to full comprehension. The person who stands on the cusp of that limitation, gazing into the depth of what can only be remotely or incompletely known, is in a position to engage in deep interreligious learning. The kind of learning that this position invites is not one of definitive propositions, but of further questions; it invites the acknowledgment of the mystery and dignity of the other.

In conclusion, let us return to the question of theological language, raised earlier in this paper. The content that is expressed by liturgical performance, in order to become communicable as theological data, must be expressed in a language appropriate to theological discourse. Given the non-propositional nature of the language of liturgical performance, translations into theological discourse are inevitably only approximate, yet the same may be said for the communication of any theological concepts. No theological reflections are entirely unmediated by cultural context and by the limitations of human comprehension and communication. Furthermore, to the religious mind, the ultimate incomprehensibility of God suggests that all theology reflects an approximate or incomplete understanding. In light of this, the obstacles present in situating interreligious dialogue and comparative theology in the context of liturgical performance may be appropriate to the ultimately incomprehensible object of theology. Given the inherent limitations, the unique language of liturgical performance may be capable of speaking theologically, and interreligiously, a message for which we ourselves cannot find words.

Notes

1. The briefer form of this adage can be interpreted in reverse ways, meaning either that liturgy forms belief, or that belief forms liturgy. This dual meaning was taken up in the 1947 encyclical *Mediator Dei*, which rejected the absolute and unequivocal formation of belief by prayer, favoring a reciprocal relationship between liturgy and doctrine. Yet, the adage most commonly refers to liturgy's formation of belief, and it is this meaning that has endured. See Clerck, Paul De "'Lex orandi, lex credendi': The Original Sense and Historical Avatars of an Equivocal Adage," *Studia Liturgica*, 24 (1994): 178–200.
2. Lindbeck, George, *The Nature of Doctrine: Religion and Theology in a Postliberal Age* (Philadelphia, PA: Westminster, 1984), p. 49.
3. Lindbeck, 48.
4. Schmemann, Alexander, "Theology and Liturgy." in *Church, World, and Mission* (Crestwood, NY: St. Vladimir's Seminary Press, 1979), p. 133.
5. Schmemann, 135.

6. Schmemann, 133–134.
7. McCall, Richard, *Do This: Liturgy as Performance* (Notre Dame, IN: University of Notre Dame Press, 2007), p. 76.
8. McCall, 69.
9. See Cornille, Catherine, *The Impossibility of Interreligious Dialogue* (New York: Herder and Herder, 2008).

CROSSCURRENTS

THE NONDUALITY OF DIVERSITY
Dialogue Among Religious Traditions

Grace Song

The proliferation of scientific civilization has brought significant improvements and conveniences to our daily life, opened lines of communication that were never before possible, and introduced a new language shaped by technological advancement. Yet, alongside human progress is the dire polarization among people, countries, and religions. Religions that once served to bring people together are now pitted against one another in the name of their founders and faith. At such a critical time, religious pluralism cannot be ignored, especially because religious diversity is apparent in almost every cosmopolitan area: Mosques built alongside churches and Christians meditating in Buddhist temples are commonplace. Efforts to promote dialogue among religions as a way to eschew ignorance are well documented, yet an underlying malaise triggers the perennial question: How is constructive and mutually beneficial dialogue possible without diminishing important differences? More importantly, how can we feel the common thread that interconnects us all, while engaging with religious diversity? In this essay, I examine these questions in light of the particular perspective on religious pluralism offered by *Won*-Buddhism (originally called the *Society for the Research of the Buddhadharma*), a Korean "new Buddhism" formed in 1916 by its founder, Sotaesan (1891–1943).

Sotaesan appeared during the turbulent and unstable period of the Japanese occupation of Korea. After years of searching for answers to his existential questions, and failing to find a teacher who could guide him, Sotaesan reached a point of complete concentration on one issue, "What should I do with this doubt?" He was plagued with doubt until one day, as he sat in absorption in the early morning, his mind was suddenly refreshed with a new energy. To verify the authenticity of this experience, he went back to all his previous questions, and the answers became clear to him. He then thought to himself that he should verify his experience by consulting texts from both Eastern and Western traditions. Shortly thereafter, he perused the Four Classics of Confucianism, *The Diamond Sutra* (*Vajracchedikā Prajñāpāramitā Sūtra* 金剛經) of Buddhism, *The Yellow Emperor's Hidden Talisman Classic* (*Huangdi Yinfujing* 黃帝陰符經) of Taoism, *The Canon of Eastern Learning* (*Donggyong daejon* 東經大全) of the Korean Tonghak religion, and the Old and New Testaments of Christianity, among others. Although his exposure to other religions was limited to what was available in Korea at the time, he believed that engaging with diverse traditions through their doctrines could lead to a holistic understanding of the fundamental principle underlying all things in the universe. Sotaesan's resulting outlook on religious pluralism was expressed as follows:

> The fundamental principles of all the world's religions are also essentially [nondual], but as different religions have long been established with different systems and expedients, there have been not a few incidents of failure to reach harmony and dialogue between these religious groups. All this is due to ignorance of the fundamental principles underlying all religions and their sects. How could this be the original intent of all the buddhas and sages?[1]

According to Sotaesan, the main cause of religious disharmony is ignorance of the nonduality of these fundamental principles—principles that are not human creations but that are given expression through religion. Stripped of religion, these principles are ineffable and beyond words and speech. Historically, charismatic religious leaders have accessed the fundamental principle underlying all things through intuitive insight and have then expressed this personal experience through language or rituals relevant to their time and location. As history shows, however, religions evolved into different forms, split into factions, and eventually misrepresent the original intent of their founders. In many cases, religious teachings take on a political role and are employed by one school to gain legitimacy over another. And so what began as the intent to convey an experience of this fundamental principle turned into strident voices vying for legitimacy and authenticity.

Sotaesan named this fundamental principle *Il-Won* (Unitary Circle) and explained that *Il-Won*

> is the original of the myriad things in heaven and earth and the realm of samādhi beyond all words and speech. Confucianism calls it the grand ultimate (*t'aegŭk*) or the ultimate of nonbeing (*mugŭk*); Daoism calls it nature or the Way (*to*); Buddhism calls it the pure Dharmakāya Buddha. In principle, however, all of these are different expressions for the same thing.[2]

Although he confines his explanation to three Eastern religious traditions, we can assume that he encompasses Western traditions in his explanation, especially in the following conversation he had with an elder of a Protestant church:

> The Founding Master said, "If a Christian becomes a disciple who truly knows Jesus, he will come also to understand what I am doing; and, if one becomes a disciple who truly understands me, he will come to understand what Jesus accomplished. Therefore, ignorant people maintain gaps between this and that religion and so think themselves to be apostate, thereby becoming hostile to other religions. However, those with real understanding know that these religions have different names merely according to the time and place, and come to view them all as belonging to a single household. Thus, you should use your own discretion whether you stay or go." Songgwang rose to his feet, bowed, and vowed anew to become his disciple. The Founding Master assented and said, "Even after you have become my disciple, you will be a true disciple of mine only when your reverence for God grows stronger."[3]

Sotaesan was confident that all great religious teachers had shared the same original intent. This intent is what the Chinese thinker Confucius (551-479 BCE) expressed as *shu* (reciprocity), or what is widely known as the ethical Golden Rule that states (in its positive form) "Always treat others as you would wish to be treated yourself." According to Sotaesan, if one understands the original intent of one sage, then the intent of all other sages becomes clear, so there is no reason to leave one religion to convert to another. Moreover, Sotaesan believed that pluralism was not relativism, but consisted of respecting others' commitments and encouraging them to investigate the original intent of the founder of their own religions. As Bokin Kim explains, when Sotaesan encountered other religious traditions, his aim was not to proselytize but to "embrace and integrate other teachings through dialogues."[4] Sotaesan used the term "single household" to indicate that different names occur merely because of differences in time and place.

The question remains: How does one truly understand the sage's intent?

Sotaesan expressed his view on this in a conversation with a Christian minister:

> The Christian minister said, "I have come to hear your good dharma-admonitions."
>
> The Founding Master said, "Then, have you been able to overcome the limits of Christianity and see the vast heaven and earth?"
>
> The minister asked, "Where is that vast heaven and earth?"
>
> The Founding Master said, "You'll find it when once you open your mind and take a broad perspective. A person who does not take a broad perspective is always preoccupied with his own affairs, and familiarizing himself only with his own traditions, criticizes others' affairs and rejects their traditions. In this way, each person cannot overcome his own norms and conventions, and will eventually fall into one-sidedness, producing gaps that become like mountains of silver and ramparts of iron. This is the reason for all the antagonisms and conflicts between countries, churches, and individuals. Why should you separate the great household that is originally perfect, and divide the great dharma that is infinite, into bits and pieces? We must abolish this gap right away, and interconnect all households to develop a full and energetic new life. Then, there will be nothing in this world that should be discarded."[5]

He told the Christian minister that to understand the intent of the sage, you need to "open your mind and take a broad perspective." By "open your mind," Sotaesan was referring to discarding dualistic ways of thinking.

One of the reasons Sotaesan was fascinated with Śākyamuni Buddha, and *The Diamond Sutra* in particular, is that they emphasize the doctrine of *no-self* and *śūnyatā* (emptiness). He expressed the experience of no-self in the following passage:

> Once enlightened to the truth of this *Won-Sang* (Circle Image), we will know that the triple worlds in the ten directions are our own property; that all things in the universe are nondual despite their different names; that this is the nature of all the buddhas, enlightened masters, ordinary humans, and sentient beings; that the principle of birth, old age, sickness, and death operates like spring, summer, autumn, and winter; that the principle of the retribution and response of cause and effect operates like the alternating predominance of *yin* and *yang*; and that this is perfect and complete, utterly impartial and selfless.[6]

According to Sotaesan, if we awaken to this fundamental principle, then although all things in the universe are different, we will know that they are nondual. This seems like such an odd way of perceiving the world: different, yet nondual? As *The Heart* Sutra famously puts this, "Form is emptiness, emptiness is form." The Japanese philosopher Keiji Nishitani (1900–1990) described true emptiness as not "something outside of and other than "being." Rather, it is to be realized as something united to and self-identical with being."[7] The "true emptiness" that Nishitani describes is what Sotaesan meant by "nature." It is precisely this "nature" that constitutes our common humanity. The Korean monk Jinul (1158–1210) explained "nature" as follows:

> From morning to evening, throughout the twelve periods of the day, during all your actions and activities—whether seeing, hearing, laughing, talking, whether angry or happy, whether doing good or evil—ultimately who is it that is able to perform all these actions? Speak! If you say that it is the physical body which is acting, then at the moment when a man's life comes to an end, even though the body has not yet decayed, how is it that the eyes cannot see, the ears cannot hear, the nose cannot smell?... You should know that what is capable of seeing, hearing, moving, and acting has to be your [nature]; it is not your physical body.[8]

Therefore our "nature" is not something supernatural or selective. As Sotaesan explained above, in terms of humans, *Il-Won* is the "nature of all the buddhas, enlightened masters, ordinary humans, and sentient beings." Although we all appear different and have different levels of knowledge and experience, our nature is nondual. For Sotaesan, this meant that a beggar and a millionaire stood apart on the level of wealth, but on the level of nature, or "original countenance," they are no different from each other. The same applies to the life cycle of birth, old age, sickness, and death. Although we come into this world and die at different times and places, the cycle we go through is the same. This is precisely the principle of the "nonduality of diversity." Yet, the fundamental problem we face—and this is true for most religions—is that we set ourselves apart from other people or other groups.

Sotaesan argues that religions fail to reach dialogue and harmony because they create barriers that separate themselves from everyone else, engendering feelings of supremacy and authority. As Nishitani writes: "To the self-centered ego of man, the world came to look like so much raw material. By wielding his great power and authority in controlling the natural world, man came to surround himself with a cold, lifeless world. Inevitably, each individual ego became like a lonely but well fortified island floating on a sea of dead matter. The life was snuffed out of nature and the things of nature; the living stream that flowed at the bottom of man and all things, and keep them bound together, dried up."[9] Nishitani here explains the predicament of self-interest having priority over the empathetic consideration of others. We are, in other words, locked in a self-bound state that ignores the essential structure of our humanity.

Religious dialogue is possible if people recognize the web of relationships, the inevitable interconnectedness they already and inevitably participate in. When we break down the walls of individuality, or "ego," something much more powerful takes over—the fount of wisdom and empathy emerge. So the Golden Rule of "Do not do to others what you would not have them do to you," naturally comes to the fore with ease and without resistance. Therefore, when Sotaesan said to the Christian minister that we need to "interconnect all households," he was suggesting that a Christian could experience meditation as taught in a Buddhist temple, and a Jewish family could invite a Muslim to partake in the richness of a Seder.

The "nonduality of diversity" means engaging with religion in a way that takes into consideration our common humanity. Sotaesan argued that religion's true purpose is to see that the Absolute does not reside somewhere far off, but that the Absolute (nature) already resides in the relative (all people and things). In the *Won*-Buddhist lexicon, this is expressed as "*Everywhere a Buddha Image, Every Act a Buddha Offering.*" He said, "Regardless of time or place, we must never neglect to maintain a respectful state of mind and pious attitude we have for the venerable Buddha. We should also exert ourselves to make buddha offerings directly to the myriad things themselves and thereby create merit and happiness in a practical manner."[10]

The same rule applies in the case of religious dialogue. Coming to the table to participate in a discussion with other religions requires a twofold commitment: Discerning the differences among traditions, and recognizing that as a rule all voices, no matter how strident they may be, arise from a common humanity. Such a commitment requires magnanimity, rectitude, and inquiry. It requires the individual to shine the light inward first before pointing the finger outward.

Sotaesan believed that the starting point for any fruitful dialogue was at the individual level. The starting point of understanding others begins by awakening to one's self-nature, which is beyond words and speech. This "nature" is no greater or better in a sage than in any other sentient being. The only difference is that when sages interact with the external world, they shine the light inward to their nature and view the world through this lens, whereas an ordinary person, unaware of this "nature," is easily pulled by habits and influenced by greed. A sage, aware of self-nature, realizes the nonduality of all things and people and therefore naturally thinks and acts out of empathy for others. There is no "I" separating the sage from the other, so everything is considered precious and every act is a gesture of gratitude.

Sotaesan believed that religious leaders play a pivotal role in helping people to realize the nonduality of the diversity of all things. In the coming age, arguing for religious dialogue on the basis of "societal duty" will not be enough to convince people of the necessity and benefits of engaging in interreligious discussion. Sotaesan believed that people had to awaken to the truth of nonduality, or no-self, and act from that experience, or else it would be mere obligation. Once we are certain that diversity is the other side of interconnectedness, then social cohesion and dialogue among religious traditions becomes a responsibility, not a choice.

Notes

1. Committee for the Authorized Translations of Won-Buddhist Scriptures, *The Scriptures of Won-Buddhism Wonbulgyo Gyojeon* (Iksan: Wonkwang Publishing, Co., 2006), 2.
2. Ibid., 143.
3. Ibid., 443-444.
4. Bokin Kim, "Dialogue and Synthesis: Sot'aesan's Perspective and Examples," *Buddhist-Christian Studies* 17 (1997): 90.
5. *The Scriptures of Won-Buddhism Wonbulgyo Gyojeon,* 314.
6. Ibid., 7.
7. Keiji Nishitani, *Religion and Nothingness* (Berkeley: University of California Press, 1982), 97.
8. Robert E. Buswell, *Tracing Back the Radiance: Chinul's Korean Way of Zen* (Honolulu: University of Hawai'i Press, 1991), 104.
9. *Religion and Nothingness*, 11.
10. *The Scriptures of Won-Buddhism Wonbulgyo Gyojeon*, 110.

CONTRIBUTORS

Yaakov Ariel is a graduate of the Hebrew University of Jerusalem and the University of Chicago, where he completed a doctoral degree on Christian messianic groups and their relation to Jews and Zionism. His research focuses on Protestant Christianity and its attitudes toward the Jewish people; on Christian–Jewish relations in the modern era; and on the Jewish reaction to modernity. Ariel has published numerous articles and two books on these subjects. His latest book, *Evangelizing the Chosen People*, was awarded the Albert C. Outler prize by the American Society of Church History. Ariel is a professor of Religious Studies at the University of North Carolina at Chapel Hill.

Todd Green is an assistant professor of religion at Luther College in Decorah, Iowa, where he teaches courses on European and American religious history. Much of his initial writing and research has concentrated on secularism and secularization in modern Europe, including his book *Responding to Secularization: The Deaconess Movement in Nineteenth-Century Sweden* (Brill, 2011). In the past few years, he has directed most of his attention to the challenges to Europe's Christian past and secular present posed by the growth and increasing visibility of Muslim minority communities in the postwar era. His particular interest is in the political mobilization against Islam by radical right political parties and the rise of Islamophobia in Europe. He contributes regularly to the religion section of *The Huffington Post* and currently co-chairs the Religion in Europe Group of the American Academy of Religion.

Lisa M. Hess, Ph.D., is a teaching elder in the Presbyterian Church (USA) and associate professor of Practical Theology and Contextual Ministries at United Seminary, one of the 13 seminaries within the United Methodist Church. She understands herself best as companion, contemplative, friend, wife, occasional preacher, and writer, most recently of *Artisanal Theology: Intentional Formation in Radically Covenantal Companionship* (Cascade 2009) and *Learning in a Musical Key: Insight for Theology in Performative Mode* (Pickwick, 2011). Her work focuses on "liturgical hospitality" and interreligious companioning at table across difference.

Katharina von Kellenbach is a professor of Religious Studies at St. Mary's College of Maryland. Her areas of expertise include feminist theology, interreligious dialogue, and Jewish–Christian relations in a post-Holocaust world. Previous publications include *Anti–Judaism in Feminist Religious Writings* (1994), essays on the first ordained female Rabbi Regina Jonas of Berlin (1902–1944), and on the theological, ethical and personal implications of the Holocaust. Her forthcoming book, *The*

Mark of Cain: Guilt and Denial in the Lives of Nazi Perpetrators (Oxford University Press), examines the effects of genocidal violence on its executioners and explores the prospects and processes of moral and spiritual recovery.

Björn Krondorfer is Director of the Martin Springer Institute at Northern Arizona University and Endowed Professor of Religious Studies in the Department of Comparative Cultural Studies. His field of expertise is religion and gender, (post-) Holocaust studies, and reconciliation studies. He is the recipient of the Norton Dodge Award for Scholarly and Creative Achievements. Publications include *Male Confessions: Intimate Revelations and the Religious Imagination* (Stanford), *Men and Masculinities in Christianity and Judaism* (London), and *Remembrance and Reconciliation* (Yale). He published three volumes in German on the cultural and theological legacy of the Holocaust. Nationally and internationally he works on reconciliation and restoration, most recently in South Africa and Israel/Palestine. He delivered the *Jerome Cardin Memorial Lecture* at Loyola University, Baltimore (2012), and the *William Temple Lecture* as the first speaker at the Jaamiatul-ilm Wal-Huda (Islamic College) in conjunction with Blackburn Cathedral, UK. He has worked together with visual artist Karen Baldner since 2003.

Mira Niculescu is a doctoral candidate at the "Ecole de Hautes Etudes en Sciences Sociales" (EHESS) in Paris with the Centre d'Etudes Interdisciplinaires du Fait Religieux (CEIFR). She was a visiting scholar at the Committee for the Study of Religion at City University of New York (CUNY) and visiting research fellow at the Hebrew University of Jerusalem (HUJ). Her doctoral research examines the contemporary mystical and contemplative developments of Judaism in the light of the "Jewish–Buddhist" phenomenon of the countercultural sixties. Her areas of interest include Jewish spirituality, Western Buddhism, Jewish Renewal, neo-Kabbalah, religious individualism and dual belongings, religious globalization, popular culture and popular religion. Publications include "Women with Shaved Heads: Western Buddhist Nuns and Haredi Jewish Wives" (in *Religion and the Body*, Abö Akademi University Press 2011) and "Mind-full of God: 'Jewish Mindfulness' as an Offspring of Buddhism in the West" (in *Buddhism without Borders*, Hawaïi University Press, forthcoming).

Emma O'Donnell is a doctoral candidate in the Ph.D. program in Comparative Theology at Boston College, working in Jewish–Christian comparative theology. She is currently writing a dissertation on the roles of memory and eschatological hope within Christian and Jewish liturgies, examining the way that the past, present, and future interact in liturgy to create a sense of transformed time. She received a B.A. from Bard College in 1998 and a Master of Theological Studies from Boston University in 2007.

Grace Song received her B.A. (Religious Studies) from the University of Toronto and M.A. (East Asian Philosophy) from Seoul National University. She is currently a Ph.D. candidate at Wonkwang University and specializes in modern Korean Buddhism. She is particularly interested in issues of sacred geography, Korean Buddhist lay movements, and Korean New Religions. Her current research includes pilgrimage to sacred Korean mountains, the Won-Buddhist perspective of the body, and tracing the origins of Won-Buddhist practice to the Āgama Sūtras. She is also the director of The One Circle Community, a non-profit organization and partner of The Charter of Compassion that hosts arts events, weekly meditation, and book clubs in Seoul.

Karla Suomala is an associate professor of Religion at Luther College in Decorah, Iowa. She received her Ph.D. from Hebrew Union College-Jewish Institute of Religion. Her teaching and research interests include Jewish–Christian–Muslim dialogue; the history of biblical interpretation with a focus on Jewish writers in the Greco-Roman and Rabbinic periods; and religion/gender studies. Karla's recent publications include "Response to Kurt Cardinal Koch," *Studies in Christian-Jewish Relations* (Vol. 7, No 1, 2012), "The Taming of Job in Judaism, Christianity, and Islam," *World & World* (Fall 2011), and "The New (con)Texts of Jewish-Christian Engagement," *Intersections* (Spring 2011). She is also the author of *Moses and God in Dialogue: Exodus 32–34 in Postbiblical Literature,* Studies in Biblical Literature, 61 (New York: Lang, 2004).

www.ingramcontent.com/pod-product-compliance
Lightning Source LLC
Chambersburg PA
CBHW040300170426
43193CB00020B/2964